Guide to Food Storage

Follow this guide for food storage, and you can be sure that what's in your freezer, refrig
ready to use in recipes.

In the Freezer (at -10° to 0° F)

DAIRY

Cheese, hard	6 months
Cheese, soft	6 months
Egg substitute, unopened	1 year
Egg whites	1 year
Egg yolks	1 year
Ice cream, sherbet	1 month

FRUITS AND VEGETABLES

Commercially frozen fruits	1 year
Commercially frozen vegetables	8 to 12 months

MEATS, POULTRY, AND SEAFOOD

Beef, Lamb, Pork, and Veal

Chops, uncooked	4 to 6 months
Ground and stew meat, uncooked	3 to 4 months
Ham, fully cooked, half	1 to 2 months
Roasts, uncooked	4 to 12 months
Steaks, uncooked	6 to 12 months

Poultry

All cuts, cooked	4 months
Boneless or bone-in pieces, uncooked	9 months

Seafood

Fish, fatty, uncooked	2 to 3 months
Fish, lean, uncooked	6 months

In the Refrigerator (at 34° to 40° F)

DAIRY

Butter	1 to 3 months
Buttermilk	1 to 2 weeks
Cheese, hard, wedge, opened	6 months
Cheese, semihard, block, opened	3 to 4 weeks
Cream cheese, fat-free, light, and ⅓-less-fat	2 weeks
Egg substitute, opened	3 days
Fresh eggs in shell	3 to 5 weeks

MEATS, POULTRY, AND SEAFOOD

Beef, Lamb, Pork, and Veal

Ground and stew meat, uncooked	1 to 2 days
Roasts, uncooked	3 to 5 days
Steaks and chops, uncooked	3 to 5 days

Chicken, Turkey, and Seafood

All cuts, uncooked	1 to 2 days

FRUITS AND VEGETABLES

Apples, beets, cabbage, carrots, celery, citrus fruits, eggplant, and parsnips	2 to 3 weeks
Apricots, asparagus, berries, cauliflower, cucumbers, mushrooms, okra, peaches, pears, peas, peppers, plums, salad greens, and summer squash	2 to 4 days
Corn, husked	1 day

In the Pantry (keep these at room temperature for 6 to 12 months)

BAKING AND COOKING STAPLES

Baking powder

Biscuit and baking mixes

Broth, canned

Cooking spray

Honey

Mayonnaise, fat-free, low-fat, and light (unopened)

Milk, canned evaporated fat-free

Milk, nonfat dry powder

Mustard, prepared (unopened)

Oils, olive and vegetable

Pasta, dried

Peanut butter

Rice, instant and regular

Salad dressings, bottled (unopened)

Seasoning sauces, bottled

Tuna, canned

FRUITS, LEGUMES, AND VEGETABLES

Fruits, canned

Legumes (beans, lentils, peas), dried or canned

Tomato products, canned

Vegetables, canned

WeightWatchers®

our best 5 ingredient

15 minute

RECIPES

Oxmoor House®

ISBN-13: 978-0-8487-3449-7
ISBN-10: 0-8487-3449-1
Library of Congress Control Number: 2011922564
Printed in the United States of America
First printing 2011

Be sure to check with your health-care provider before making any changes in your diet.

Weight Watchers is a registered trademark of Weight Watchers International, Inc. ***PointsPlus*™** is the trademark of Weight Watchers International, Inc. Trademarks are used under license by Time Home Entertainment Inc.

Oxmoor House

VP, Publishing Director: Jim Childs
Editorial Director: Susan Payne Dobbs
Brand Manager: Victoria Alfonso
Senior Editor: Heather Averett
Managing Editor: Laurie S. Herr

Weight Watchers® Our Best 5 Ingredient 15 Minute Recipes

Project Editors: Diane Rose, Holly D. Smith
Senior Designer: Melissa Jones Clark
Assistant Designer: Allison L. Sperando
Director, Test Kitchens: Elizabeth Tyler Austin
Assistant Directors, Test Kitchens: Julie Christopher, Julie Gunter
Test Kitchens Professionals: Wendy Ball, Allison E. Cox, Victoria E. Cox, Margaret Monroe Dickey,
      Alyson Moreland Haynes, Stefanie Maloney, Callie Nash, Kathleen Royal Phillips,
      Catherine Crowell Steele, Ashley T. Strickland, Leah Van Deren
Photography Director: Jim Bathie
Assistant Photo Stylist: Mary Louise Menendez
Production Manager: Theresa Beste-Farley

Contributors

Copy Editor: Dolores Hydock
Proofreader: Julie Gillis
Indexer: Mary Ann Laurens
Nutritional Analysis: Caroline Glagola
Interns: Sarah H. Doss, Blair Gillespie, Elizabeth Nelson, Caitlin Watzke
Photographers: Beau Gustafson, Mary Britton Senseney
Photo Stylists: Missy Neville Crawford, Mindy Shapiro

Cover: Balsamic Chicken with Roasted Tomatoes (page 89)

To order additional publications, call
1-800-765-6400.
For more books to enrich your life, visit
oxmoorhouse.com

To search, savor, and share
thousands of recipes, visit
myrecipes.com

Contents

Secrets for Great Meals in Minutes

Recipes with short ingredient lists and straightforward procedures depend on quality ingredients. Choose your ingredients carefully, follow a few simple strategies, and you, too, can master the art of quick cooking. First, start with fresh, quick-cooking proteins, such as fish fillets, pork chops, lamb chops, ground beef, and chicken breast halves. Combine these with fresh fruits, vegetables, and herbs, plus a few high-quality, high-flavor convenience foods. Rely on cooking methods that can produce flavorful results fast, such as sautéing or broiling. Finally, pair the dish with a simple side or an easy dessert.

9 Super Shortcuts

1. **Keep your pantry, fridge, and freezer well stocked** with commonly used food items to avoid last-minute shopping trips for missing ingredients. By storing a supply of basic, non-perishable items, you can improvise main- and side-dish recipes when needed.

2. **Save prep and cook time** by using convenient potato products, such as refrigerated or frozen wedges, quarters, hash browns, and mashed potatoes. If you're using fresh potatoes, leave the skin on to save prep time and to preserve nutrients and fiber.

3. **Forgo coring, peeling, and slicing fresh fruit** yourself. Look in the produce section for presliced apple; seeded or unseeded melon chunks; cored pineapple; and bottles of sliced fresh citrus sections, mango, and papaya.

4. **Keep bottled whole peeled garlic cloves** on hand to add flavor to meats or side dishes.

5. **Gather and prepare all of your ingredients** and utensils before you start cooking. This will reduce the number of trips to your cabinets and refrigerator to dig for ingredients and tools at the last minute.

6. **To bring water to a boil more quickly,** preheat the pan on the stove, start with hot tap water, and cover the pot until the water reaches the boiling point.

7. While you may have to pay a little extra, **buying peeled and deveined shrimp** is a real time-saver. Ask someone in your seafood department to cook your shrimp while you finish your grocery shopping.

8. Simplify side dishes by **using quick-cooking pastas and grains** such as couscous, quick-cooking grits, precooked microwaveable rice, and fresh pasta.

9. **Eliminate chopping and slicing** vegetables by using packaged prechopped vegetables from the produce section of your supermarket, such as broccoli florets, carrots, celery, mixed stir-fry vegetables, and onion.

The 15-Minute Pantry

We use these ingredients and convenience products to shave time off of recipes. Keep them on hand, and your next meal is only minutes away.

Staple Pantry Items

- ❑ Alcohol and liqueurs: beer, bourbon, Grand Marnier (orange-flavored liqueur), rum, and wine
- ❑ Anchovy paste
- ❑ Balsamic glaze
- ❑ Bottled roasted red bell peppers
- ❑ Breadcrumbs: dry and panko
- ❑ Broth: fat-free, lower-sodium beef, chicken, and vegetable
- ❑ Canned beans: black, cannellini, garbanzo, kidney, and navy
- ❑ Canned or packaged tuna
- ❑ Capers
- ❑ Chile paste and curry paste
- ❑ Chipotle chiles in adobo sauce
- ❑ Chutneys
- ❑ Cooking spray: regular, butter-flavored, and olive oil–flavored
- ❑ Dried fruits and vegetables: cranberries, figs, raisins, and sun-dried tomatoes
- ❑ Dried herbs, spices, and spice blends
- ❑ Extracts: almond and vanilla
- ❑ Grains: barley, bulgur, quick-cooking oats, grits, and polenta
- ❑ Honey and syrups: regular and lavender honey; chocolate and maple syrup
- ❑ Jams, jellies, and preserves
- ❑ Ketchup
- ❑ Mayonnaise: light and reduced-fat
- ❑ Mustard: Dijon, prepared, and whole-grain Dijon
- ❑ Nuts: almonds, hazelnuts, peanuts, pecans, pine nuts, pistachios, and walnuts
- ❑ Oil: canola, dark sesame, extra-virgin olive, and olive
- ❑ Olives: black, green, and kalamata
- ❑ Pastas: angel hair, couscous, farfalle, orzo, penne, rotini, soba, and spaghetti
- ❑ Pasta sauce
- ❑ Relishes: dill pickle and sweet pickle
- ❑ Rice: Arborio, basmati, brown, jasmine, long-grain, white, and wild
- ❑ Salad dressings
- ❑ Sauces: barbecue, chili, fish, hoisin, lower-sodium soy, picante, and Worcestershire
- ❑ Sugars: dark and light brown, granulated, powdered, and turbinado
- ❑ Tomato products, canned
- ❑ Vinegars: balsamic, Champagne, cider, red wine, rice, sherry, white balsamic, and white wine

Produce Department

- ❑ Bagged salad and salad mixes
- ❑ Fresh fruits, herbs, and vegetables
- ❑ Fresh garlic and ginger
- ❑ Fresh salsa
- ❑ Lemons, limes, and oranges
- ❑ Pesto
- ❑ Prechopped vegetables and vegetable mixes
- ❑ Tofu, extra-firm

Dairy Case

- ❑ Butter
- ❑ Cheeses: Asiago, blue, cheddar, cheddar-Jack, cream cheese, feta, Fontina, goat, Jarlsberg, mascarpone, Mexican blend, Monterey Jack, mozzarella, Muenster, Parmesan, pepper-Jack, provolone, queso fresco, and Swiss
- ❑ Milk: low-fat and nonfat buttermilk, fat-free, half-and-half, 1% low-fat, 2% reduced-fat, whole
- ❑ Sour cream: light and reduced-fat
- ❑ Yogurt-based spread
- ❑ Yogurt: lemon meringue light, fat-free Greek, plain fat-free, and vanilla fat-free

Refrigerated Section

- ❑ Eggs
- ❑ Egg substitute
- ❑ Fresh pasta
- ❑ Fresh pasta sauce

Deli, Meat, and Seafood Counter

- ❑ Bacon
- ❑ Beef: ground, roasts, steaks, and tenderloin
- ❑ Chicken: breast cutlets, drumsticks, rotisserie, skinless breast halves, tenders, and thighs
- ❑ Deli meats: ham, roast beef, and turkey
- ❑ Fresh fish and shellfish: catfish, flounder, grouper, halibut, littleneck clams, lump crab meat, orange roughy, red snapper, salmon, sea scallops, shrimp, tilapia, trout, and tuna steaks
- ❑ Lamb: ground and loin chops
- ❑ Pork: chops and tenderloin
- ❑ Sausage: hot turkey Italian sausage and turkey breakfast sausage
- ❑ Turkey, ground

Freezer Case

- ❑ Frozen fish and seafood
- ❑ Frozen fruits and vegetables
- ❑ Ice cream

Want to Learn More about Weight Watchers?

Weight Watchers is a recognized leader in weight management that has been helping people successfully lose weight for more than 45 years. At Weight Watchers, weight management is a partnership that combines our knowledge with your efforts. Our weight-loss plan reflects sound and up-to-date scientific research. You'll find an integrated approach that offers good eating choices, healthy habits, a supportive environment, and exercise. For more information about the Weight Watchers program and a meeting nearest you, call 1-800-651-6000 or visit online at www.weightwatchers.com

About the Recipes

Weight Watchers® *Our Best 5 Ingredient 15 Minute Recipes* gives you the nutrition facts you need to stay on track. Every recipe in this book requires five ingredients or less (excluding water, cooking spray, salt, pepper, and optional ingredients) or can be prepared in 15 minutes or less. Each recipe also includes a *PointsPlus*™ value. For more information on Weight Watchers, see page 5.

Each recipe has a list of nutrients—including calories, fat, saturated fat, protein, carbohydrates, dietary fiber, cholesterol, iron, sodium, and calcium—as well as a serving size and the number of servings. This information makes it easy for you to use the recipes for any weight-loss program that you choose to follow. Measurements are abbreviated g (grams) and mg (milligrams). Nutritional values used in our calculations come from either The Food Processor, Version 8.9 (ESHA Research), or are provided by food manufacturers.

Numbers are based on these assumptions:
• Unless otherwise indicated, meat, poultry, and fish always refer to skinned, boned, and cooked servings.
• When we give a range for an ingredient (3 to 3½ cups flour, for instance), we calculate using the lesser amount.
• Some alcohol calories evaporate during heating; the analysis reflects this.
• Only the amount of marinade absorbed by the food is used in calculations.
• Garnishes and optional ingredients are not included in an analysis.

Safety Note: Cooking spray should never be used near direct heat. Always remove a pan from heat before spraying it with cooking spray.

A Note on Diabetic Exchanges: You may notice that the nutrient analysis for each recipe does not include Diabetic Exchanges. Most dietitians and diabetes educators are now teaching people with diabetes to count total carbohydrates at each meal and snack, rather than counting exchanges. Counting carbohydrates gives people with diabetes more flexibility in their food choices and seems to be an effective way to manage blood glucose.

PointsPlus values

PointsPlus uses the latest scientific research to create a program that goes far beyond traditional calorie counting to give people the edge they need to lose weight and keep it off in a fundamentally healthier way. The Program is designed to educate and encourage people to make choices that focus on foods that create a sense of satisfaction and are more healthful. *PointsPlus* values are calculated for foods based on their protein, fiber, fat, and carbohydrate content. This *PointsPlus* formula takes into account how these nutrients are processed by the body and helps you select foods that are both nutritious and satisfying! For more about the *PointsPlus* Program, visit WeightWatchers.com.

Breakfast

pictured on page 34

Pecan-Apple Sticky Buns

prep: 4 minutes • **cook:** 20 minutes • **other:** 1 minute
PointsPlus value per serving: 6

Refrigerated canned cinnamon roll dough gets special treatment by adding a gooey apple and pecan topping. We love serving it for breakfast, but it also makes a great dessert. Without a doubt, your breakfast or dinner guests will be thrilled!

1½   cups finely chopped peeled apple (about 1 large apple)
 ½   cup chopped pecans
 ¼   cup packed brown sugar
 3   tablespoons 5⁵⁄₅₀ non-hydrogenated buttery blend stick spread (such as Smart Balance)
Cooking spray
 1   (12.4-ounce) can refrigerated reduced-fat cinnamon roll dough

1. Preheat oven to 400°.
2. Place first 4 ingredients in a 9-inch round baking pan coated with cooking spray. Bake at 400° for 4 minutes or until butter melts. Spread mixture evenly over bottom of pan.
3. Open cinnamon roll can; reserve icing for another use, or discard. Arrange cinnamon rolls over apple mixture in pan. Bake at 400° for 16 minutes or until golden brown. Cool rolls in pan 1 minute. Invert pan onto a serving platter. Serve immediately. **Yield:** 8 servings (serving size: 1 sticky bun).

Per serving: CALORIES 221; FAT 11.6g (sat 3.2g, mono 3.9g, poly 2.8g); PROTEIN 2.7g; CARB 29g; FIBER 1g; CHOL 1mg; IRON 1mg; SODIUM 375mg; CALC 12mg

---

Menu
PointsPlus value per serving: 8

Pecan-Apple Sticky Bun

1 cup fat-free milk
PointsPlus value per serving: 2

Game Plan

1. Peel and chop apple.

2. Assemble and bake sticky buns.

Biscuits with Orange Butter and Strawberries

prep: 4 minutes • **cook:** 10 minutes   *PointsPlus* value per serving: 2

Buttery spread tinged with orange rind and fresh strawberries dresses up an ordinary canned biscuit. These simple additions take these biscuits from simple to spectacular.

    1 (7.5-ounce) can refrigerated buttermilk biscuit dough
    3 tablespoons 5%⁄₀ non-hydrogenated buttery blend stick spread
       (such as Smart Balance)
    2 tablespoons powdered sugar
    1 teaspoon grated orange rind
    1 cup sliced strawberries

1. Preheat oven to 450°.
2. Bake biscuits at 450° according to package directions.
3. While biscuits bake, combine spread, powdered sugar, and orange rind, stirring with a fork until smooth.
4. Split biscuits; spread evenly with buttery spread mixture, and top with sliced strawberries. **Yield:** 10 servings (serving size: 1 biscuit, 1½ teaspoons orange butter, and about 1½ tablespoons strawberries).

Per serving: CALORIES 87; FAT 3.5g (sat 1g, mono 1.1g, poly 0.8g); PROTEIN 1.5g; CARB 13g; FIBER 0.7g; CHOL 0mg; IRON 0.6mg; SODIUM 217mg; CALC 3mg

Menu
PointsPlus value per serving: 3

Biscuit with Orange Butter and Strawberries

1 slice Canadian bacon
PointsPlus value per serving: 1

Game Plan

1. While biscuits bake:
   • Grate orange rind.
   • Wash and slice strawberries.
   • Mix spread.

2. Heat Canadian bacon according to package directions.

3. Assemble biscuits.

Menu
PointsPlus value
per serving: 9

**Oatmeal with Walnuts and
Apple Butter**

**1 (6-ounce) carton French
vanilla fat-free yogurt**
PointsPlus value per
serving: 4

Game Plan

1. While oats cook:
  • Toast walnuts.

2. Assemble oatmeal in
   individual bowls.

Oatmeal with Walnuts and Apple Butter

prep: 2 minutes • **cook:** 19 minutes *PointsPlus* value per serving: 5

Steel-cut oats provide similar nutritional benefits to rolled oats but have a heartier texture and distinct nutty flavor.

  1 cup steel-cut oats (such as McCann's)
  ⅛ teaspoon salt
  3 cups water
  ½ cup apple butter
  2 tablespoons brown sugar
  ¼ teaspoon ground cinnamon
  ¼ cup chopped walnuts, toasted

1. Combine first 3 ingredients in a medium saucepan; bring to a boil. Reduce heat; simmer, uncovered, 15 minutes or until desired consistency, stirring occasionally. Remove from heat. Stir in apple butter, brown sugar, and cinnamon. Divide oatmeal evenly among 4 bowls; sprinkle each serving with walnuts. **Yield:** 4 servings (serving size: ¾ cup oatmeal and 1 tablespoon walnuts).

Per serving: CALORIES 200; FAT 6.1g (sat 0.7g, mono 1.2g, poly 4g); PROTEIN 3.8g; CARB 34g; FIBER 3g; CHOL 0mg; IRON 1.3mg; SODIUM 86mg; CALC 23mg

pictured on page 33

Southwestern Breakfast Wraps

prep: 4 minutes • **cook:** 8 minutes   *PointsPlus* value per serving: 7

Start your day with a hearty wrap packed with protein.

- 4 ounces hot turkey Italian sausage
- 3 large eggs
- 3 large egg whites
- 2 tablespoons fat-free milk
- ¼ teaspoon salt
- ⅛ teaspoon black pepper
- Cooking spray
- 4 (8-inch) low-carb whole-wheat flour tortillas, warmed (such as Mission Carb Balance)
- 1 cup (4 ounces) shredded reduced-fat colby-Jack cheese
- ½ cup refrigerated fresh salsa

1. Brown sausage in a large nonstick skillet; drain, and remove from pan.

2. Combine whole eggs and next 4 ingredients in a small bowl, stirring well with a whisk. Heat a medium nonstick skillet over medium-high heat. Coat pan with cooking spray. Add egg mixture; cook, stirring occasionally, until eggs are set.

3. Spoon eggs evenly onto center of each tortilla; sprinkle evenly with sausage, and top with cheese. Roll up. Serve with salsa. **Yield:** 4 servings (serving size: 1 wrap and 2 tablespoons salsa).

Per serving: CALORIES 305; FAT 14.6g (sat 6.1g, mono 2.5g, poly 1.3g); PROTEIN 24g; CARB 22g; FIBER 11g; CHOL 183mg; IRON 1.8mg; SODIUM 972mg; CALC 292mg

---

Menu
PointsPlus value per serving: 7

Southwestern Breakfast Wrap

1 cup seedless red grapes
PointsPlus value per serving: 0

Game Plan

1. While sausage browns:
- Combine egg mixture.
- Warm tortillas.

2. Cook eggs.

3. Assemble wraps.

Eggs Florentine Waffle Stack

prep: 3 minutes • **cook:** 12 minutes

PointsPlus value per serving: 10

Game Plan

1. While waffles toast:
   • Rinse spinach.

2. Heat milk and cheese; wilt spinach.

3. Combine and cook eggs.

4. Assemble waffle stack.

This is an impressive recipe for brunch. Serve with fresh fruit for a complete meal.

¾ cup plus 1 tablespoon 1% low-fat milk, divided
1   tablespoon all-purpose flour
½   cup (2 ounces) shredded Swiss cheese
⅛   teaspoon salt
⅛   teaspoon black pepper
2   cups bagged baby spinach leaves
1   teaspoon yogurt-based spread (such as Brummel & Brown)
2   large eggs
2   large egg whites
Cooking spray
2   (1.7-ounce) frozen multigrain waffles (such as Van's), toasted
1   precooked bacon slice, crumbled

1. Combine ¾ cup milk and flour in a small saucepan, stirring with a whisk until smooth. Cook over medium heat 2 to 3 minutes or until thick and bubbly. Add cheese, salt, and pepper, stirring until cheese melts. Add spinach and yogurt-based spread, stirring until spinach wilts.

2. Combine eggs, egg whites, and remaining 1 tablespoon milk, stirring with a whisk. Heat a small nonstick skillet over medium-high heat. Coat pan with cooking spray. Add egg mixture; cook 2 minutes, stirring slowly and frequently.

3. Spoon creamed spinach evenly over waffles; top with eggs, and sprinkle with crumbled bacon. **Yield:** 2 servings (serving size: 1 waffle, ½ cup spinach mixture, ½ of egg mixture, and ½ slice bacon).

Per serving: CALORIES 384; FAT 20.3g (sat 8.2g, mono 5.2g, poly 1.6g); PROTEIN 25g; CARB 28g; FIBER 4g; CHOL 247mg; IRON 3mg; SODIUM 674mg; CALC 400mg

Roasted Pepper, Ham, Potato, and Havarti Omelet

prep: 6 minutes • **cook:** 8 minutes   **PointsPlus** value per serving: 9

This loaded omelet makes a great "breakfast for dinner" option, too.

  1   cup diced red potato
  1   tablespoon butter
  ½   cup vertically sliced sweet onion
      Cooking spray
  1   cup egg substitute
  ¼   teaspoon freshly ground black pepper
  ⅛   teaspoon salt
  ½   cup sliced bottled roasted red bell peppers
  2   ounces shaved deli lower-sodium ham (such as Boar's Head)
  ¼   cup (1 ounce) shredded reduced-fat Havarti cheese

1. Place potato in a small microwave-safe bowl. Cover with plastic wrap; vent. Microwave at HIGH 3 minutes or until tender.

2. While potato cooks, melt butter in a large nonstick skillet over medium-high heat. Add onion; sauté 2 minutes or until tender. Remove from pan; add to potato.

3. Return pan to medium heat; coat pan with cooking spray. Combine egg substitute, black pepper, and salt; stir well with a whisk. Pour egg mixture into pan, and let egg mixture set slightly (do not stir). Carefully loosen set edges of omelet with a spatula, tipping the pan to pour uncooked egg to the sides. Continue this procedure for about 10 to 15 seconds or until almost no runny egg remains.

4. Spoon potato mixture, bell pepper, and ham over half of omelet; top mixture with cheese. Run spatula around edges and under omelet to loosen it from pan; fold in half. Carefully slide omelet from pan onto a serving plate. Cut omelet in half; serve immediately. **Yield:** 2 servings (serving size: ½ of omelet).

Per serving: CALORIES 353; FAT 16.1g (sat 4.5g, mono 2.7g, poly 2.3g); PROTEIN 31g; CARB 20g; FIBER 2g; CHOL 39mg; IRON 4mg; SODIUM 911mg; CALC 291mg

Menu
PointsPlus value
per serving: 9

Roasted Pepper, Ham, Potato, and Havarti Omelet

Game Plan

1. Wash and dice potato.

2. Slice and sauté onion.

3. Combine and cook egg mixture.

4. Add filling to omelet and top with grated cheese.

Chile Relleño Egg Bake

prep: 6 minutes • **cook:** 45 minutes   *PointsPlus* value per serving: 4

All the key ingredients of a chile relleño are combined in this easy breakfast casserole.

 1 cup fat-free milk
 3 large eggs
 3 large egg whites
 1 (8¾-ounce) can whole-kernel corn, drained
 1 (4.5-ounce) can chopped green chiles, drained
 ½ cup (2 ounces) reduced-fat shredded cheddar cheese
 Cooking spray
 Refrigerated fresh salsa (optional)

1. Preheat oven to 325°.

2. Combine first 3 ingredients in a bowl, stirring well with a whisk. Stir in corn, chiles, and cheese. Pour into an 8-inch square baking dish coated with cooking spray.

3. Bake at 325° for 45 minutes or until set. Serve with salsa, if desired. **Yield:** 4 servings (serving size: ¼ of casserole).

Per serving: CALORIES 160; FAT 5.5g (sat 1.8g, mono 1.8g, poly 0.6g); PROTEIN 14g; CARB 12g; FIBER 0.9g; CHOL 163mg; IRON 1mg; SODIUM 454mg; CALC 157mg

---

Menu
PointsPlus value
per serving: 7

Chile Relleño Egg Bake

1 whole-wheat English muffin
PointsPlus value
per serving: 3

Game Plan

1. While oven preheats:
  • Drain corn and chiles.
  • Prepare egg mixture.

2. While dish is cooking:
  • Toast English muffin.

Breakfast Monte Cristo

prep: 4 minutes • **cook:** 10 minutes   *PointsPlus* value per serving: 7

A traditional Monte Cristo sandwich is made with Swiss cheese, but we liked milder provolone for a breakfast option.

Butter-flavored cooking spray
2   (0.5-ounce) slices Canadian bacon
2   (0.6-ounce) slices reduced-fat provolone cheese
2   (2-ounce) double-fiber honey-wheat English muffins
1   large egg
⅛   teaspoon salt
⅛   teaspoon black pepper
1½   teaspoons powdered sugar
¼   cup low-sugar orange marmalade

1. Heat a large nonstick skillet over medium-high heat. Coat pan with cooking spray. Add Canadian bacon; cook 2 minutes on each side or until lightly browned. Place 1 slice each of Canadian bacon and provolone cheese on bottom of each English muffin. Top with English muffin tops.

2. Combine egg, salt, and pepper, stirring with a whisk. Dip each sandwich into egg mixture, allowing excess to drip off. Heat a large nonstick skillet over medium heat. Coat pan with cooking spray. Add sandwiches to pan. Cook 3 minutes on each side or until lightly browned and cheese melts. Sprinkle each sandwich with powdered sugar. Place orange marmalade in a small microwave-safe bowl; microwave at HIGH 30 seconds or until melted. Serve with sandwiches. **Yield:** 2 servings (serving size: 1 sandwich and 2 tablespoons orange marmalade).

Per serving: CALORIES 268; FAT 7g (sat 2.9g, mono 2.4g, poly 0.6g); PROTEIN 14g; CARB 40.3g; FIBER 5g; CHOL 122mg; IRON 2.1mg; SODIUM 669mg; CALC 229mg

Menu
PointsPlus value per serving: 7

Breakfast Monte Cristo

1 orange
PointsPlus value per serving: 0

Game Plan

1. While Canadian bacon cooks:
  • Prepare egg wash.

2. Assemble and cook sandwiches.

Menu

PointsPlus value
per serving: 9

Cinnamon-Swirl Pancakes
with "Buttercream Icing"

Game Plan

1. Prepare pancake batter.

2. While pancakes cook:
   • Prepare buttercream
     mixture.

Cinnamon-Swirl Pancakes with "Buttercream Icing"

prep: 4 minutes • **cook:** 10 minutes   *PointsPlus* value per serving: 9

If you like cinnamon rolls slathered with buttercream icing, you'll love these pancakes, swirled with cinnamon. We top them with a drizzle that tastes like buttercream icing.

1½ cups low-fat baking mix
  2 tablespoons granulated sugar
⅔ cup nonfat buttermilk
¼ cup egg substitute
¾ teaspoon ground cinnamon
    Cooking spray
1½ cups powdered sugar
  1 tablespoon light butter, melted
  2 tablespoons 1% low-fat milk
½ teaspoon vanilla extract

1. Lightly spoon baking mix into dry measuring cups; level with a knife. Combine baking mix and granulated sugar in a medium bowl, stirring with a whisk.
2. Combine buttermilk and egg substitute, and add to dry mixture, stirring until smooth. Stir in cinnamon.
3. Heat a nonstick griddle or nonstick skillet over medium heat. Coat pan with cooking spray. Pour about ¼ cup batter per pancake onto pan. Cook 3 minutes or until tops are covered with bubbles and edges look cooked. Carefully turn pancakes over; cook 2 minutes or until bottoms are lightly browned.
4. While pancakes cook, combine powdered sugar, butter, milk, and vanilla; stir with a whisk. Drizzle over warm pancakes. **Yield:** 5 servings (serving size: 2 pancakes and about 1½ tablespoons "buttercream icing").

Per serving: CALORIES 326; FAT 4.2g (sat 0.8g, mono 1.5g, poly 0.7g); PROTEIN 5.7g; CARB 68g; FIBER 0.7g; CHOL 3.8mg; IRON 1.6mg; SODIUM 467mg; CALC 194mg

Fish & Shellfish

Menu

PointsPlus value
per serving: 7

Grilled Amberjack with
Country-Style Dijon Cream
Sauce

½ cup steamed asparagus
PointsPlus value
per serving: 0

1 (½-inch) slice whole-wheat
baguette
PointsPlus value
per serving: 1

Game Plan

1. While grill heats:
   • Rub fillets with season-
     ing mixture.
   • Steam asparagus.
2. While fish cooks:
   • Prepare sauce.

Grilled Amberjack with Country-Style Dijon Cream Sauce

prep: 2 minutes • **cook:** 7 minutes   *PointsPlus* value per serving: 6

Prepare the cream sauce ahead, if you like—just be sure to reserve the lemon juice for the fish. Pick up a whole-wheat baguette from the bakery at your supermarket, and steam fresh asparagus to make this meal quick and easy.

  2   teaspoons salt-free steak grilling blend (such as Mrs. Dash)
1½   teaspoons chopped fresh tarragon
    Cooking spray
  4   (6-ounce) amberjack fillets (about ¾ inch thick)
  1   lemon
    Country-Style Dijon Cream Sauce

1. Combine steak seasoning and tarragon in a small bowl; set aside.
2. Heat a grill pan over medium-high heat. Coat pan with cooking spray. Coat fillets with cooking spray, and rub with seasoning mixture. Add fish to pan. Cook 3 to 4 minutes on each side or until desired degree of doneness.
3. While fish cooks, grate 1 teaspoon rind from lemon; squeeze juice to measure 1 tablespoon. Reserve lemon rind for Country-Style Dijon Cream Sauce.
4. Place 1 fillet on each of 4 plates. Drizzle fillets evenly with lemon juice, and top with a dollop of cream sauce. **Yield:** 4 servings (serving size: 1 fillet, about ¾ teaspoon lemon juice, and 3 tablespoons cream sauce).

Per serving: CALORIES 256; FAT 8g (sat 0.8g, mono 4g, poly 3g); PROTEIN 37.2g; CARB 6.3g; FIBER 0.6g; CHOL 83mg; IRON 0.1mg; SODIUM 473mg; CALC 39mg

Country-Style Dijon Cream Sauce

prep: 4 minutes   *PointsPlus* value per serving: 2

  ¼   cup light mayonnaise
  ¼   cup fat-free sour cream
  3   tablespoons water
1½   tablespoons country-style Dijon mustard
1½   teaspoons chopped fresh tarragon
  1   teaspoon grated lemon rind
  ¼   teaspoon salt

1. Combine all ingredients in a small bowl. **Yield:** 4 servings (serving size: 3 tablespoons).

Per serving: CALORIES 71; FAT 4.9g (sat 0.8g, mono 1g, poly 2.5g); PROTEIN 1.1g; CARB 5g; FIBER 0.1g; CHOL 8mg; IRON 0.1mg; SODIUM 413mg; CALC 33mg

Baked Bayou Catfish with Spicy Sour Cream Sauce

prep: 5 minutes • **cook:** 14 minutes   *PointsPlus* value per serving: 8

Cooking spray
½   cup yellow cornmeal
2½ tablespoons hot sauce, divided
4   (6-ounce) catfish fillets
1   teaspoon Cajun seasoning (such as Luzianne)
½   cup light sour cream
⅛   teaspoon salt
1   lemon, cut into wedges (optional)
Chopped fresh parsley (optional)

1. Preheat oven to 400°.
2. Line a large baking sheet with foil; coat foil with cooking spray.
3. Place cornmeal in a shallow dish. Brush 1½ tablespoons hot sauce evenly on both sides of fillets; sprinkle with Cajun seasoning, and dredge in cornmeal, pressing gently. Place fillets on prepared pan. Coat fillets with cooking spray. Bake at 400° for 14 minutes or until desired degree of doneness.
4. While fillets bake, combine remaining 1 tablespoon hot sauce, sour cream, and salt in a small bowl, stirring with a whisk. Serve fillets with sauce and lemon wedges, if desired. Sprinkle with parsley, if desired. **Yield:** 4 servings (serving size: 1 fillet and 2 tablespoons sauce).

Per serving: CALORIES 322; FAT 15.7g (sat 4.6g, mono 6.2g, poly 4.9g); PROTEIN 28.7g; CARB 15.7g; FIBER 1.3g; CHOL 90mg; IRON 2.1mg; SODIUM 524mg; CALC 77mg

Menu
POINTSPLUS value per serving: 10

Baked Bayou Catfish with Spicy Sour Cream Sauce

Sweet-and-Sour Broccoli Slaw

Game Plan

1. While oven preheats:
• Season and coat fish.

2. While fish cooks:
• Prepare Spicy Sour Cream Sauce.
• Assemble Sweet-and-Sour Broccoli Slaw.

Sweet-and-Sour Broccoli Slaw

prep: 4 minutes   *PointsPlus* value per serving: 2

1   tablespoon sugar
2   tablespoons cider vinegar
1   tablespoon canola oil
¼   teaspoon poppy seeds
⅛   teaspoon salt
⅛   teaspoon freshly ground black pepper
Dash of ground red pepper
2½ cups packaged broccoli coleslaw

1. Combine first 7 ingredients in a medium bowl, stirring with a whisk. Add coleslaw; toss well. Serve immediately. **Yield:** 4 servings (serving size: about ⅔ cup).

Per serving: CALORIES 62; FAT 3.6g (sat 0.3g, mono 2.1g, poly 1.1g); PROTEIN 1.3g; CARB 5.7g; FIBER 1.3g; CHOL 0mg; IRON 0.4mg; SODIUM 88mg; CALC 14mg

Menu
PointsPlus value
per serving: 7

Blackened Catfish

Sautéed Corn and Cherry Tomatoes

Game Plan

1. Wash and chop corn, cherry tomatoes, and green onions.

2. While fish cooks:
• Prepare Sautéed Corn and Cherry Tomatoes.

Blackened Catfish

prep: 3 minutes • **cook:** 9 minutes   *PointsPlus* value per serving: 5

A combination of a few pantry spices lends authentic Cajun flavor to catfish. The Sautéed Corn and Cherry Tomatoes are delicious served alone as a side dish or as a relish spooned over the catfish.

    1   tablespoon fresh thyme leaves, minced
    1   teaspoon onion powder
    1   teaspoon garlic powder
    1   teaspoon paprika
    1   teaspoon black pepper
    ½   teaspoon ground red pepper
    ¼   teaspoon salt
    3   teaspoons olive oil, divided
    4   (6-ounce) catfish fillets

1. Combine first 7 ingredients in a small bowl.

2. Heat a large nonstick skillet over medium-high heat. Add 2 teaspoons oil to pan. Brush fillets with remaining 1 teaspoon olive oil. Rub fillets with spice mixture, and add to pan; cook 3 minutes on each side or until desired degree of doneness. **Yield:** 4 servings (serving size: 1 fillet).

Per serving: CALORIES 200; FAT 8.3g (sat 1.7g, mono 3.9g, poly 1.9g); PROTEIN 28.2g; CARB 1.9g; FIBER 0.5g; CHOL 99mg; IRON 0.9mg; SODIUM 220mg; CALC 37mg

Sautéed Corn and Cherry Tomatoes

prep: 4 minutes • **cook:** 6 minutes   *PointsPlus* value per serving: 2

    2   teaspoons olive oil
    1   garlic clove, minced
    2   cups fresh corn kernels (about 3 ears)
    1   cup cherry tomatoes, quartered (about 10)
    3   tablespoons chopped green onions (about 2 large)
    1   tablespoon sherry vinegar
    2   teaspoons minced fresh thyme
    ½   teaspoon freshly ground black pepper
    ¼   teaspoon salt

1. Heat oil in a large nonstick skillet over medium heat. Add garlic to pan; sauté 1 minute. Add corn and tomatoes; cook 3 minutes or until vegetables are tender, stirring often. Remove from heat; stir in onions and remaining ingredients. **Yield:** 4 servings (serving size: about ½ cup).

Per serving: CALORIES 89; FAT 3.2g (sat 0.5g, mono 1.9g, poly 0.7g); PROTEIN 2.6g; CARB 15g; FIBER 2.4g; CHOL 0mg; IRON 0.7mg; SODIUM 158mg; CALC 12mg

Baked Flounder with Dill and Caper Cream

prep: 8 minutes • **cook:** 12 minutes

PointsPlus value per serving: 5

Fresh dill contributes sharp flavor and feathery elegance to this simple flounder recipe. Since heat diminishes the potency of fresh dill, it's best to add it to the dish near the end of the suggested cooking time.

- ¼ teaspoon black pepper
- ⅛ teaspoon salt
- 4 (6-ounce) flounder fillets
- Cooking spray
- 1 tablespoon chopped fresh dill
- ½ cup reduced-fat sour cream
- 2 tablespoons capers, drained
- 4 lemon wedges

1. Preheat oven to 425°.

2. Sprinkle pepper and salt evenly over fillets. Place fish on a foil-lined baking sheet coated with cooking spray. Bake at 425° for 10 minutes; sprinkle evenly with dill. Bake an additional 2 minutes or until desired degree of doneness.

3. While fish bakes, combine sour cream and capers in a small bowl. Place fish on a serving platter. Squeeze 1 lemon wedge over each fillet. Serve with caper cream.
Yield: 4 servings (serving size: 1 fillet and about 2 tablespoons cream).

Per serving: CALORIES 205; FAT 6g (sat 2.9g, mono 0.4g, poly 0.6g); PROTEIN 33.6g; CARB 2.8g; FIBER 0.2g; CHOL 97mg; IRON 0.7mg; SODIUM 356mg; CALC 83mg

Menu
PointsPlus value per serving: 8

Baked Flounder with Dill and Caper Cream

½ cup precooked brown rice
PointsPlus value per serving: 3

½ cup steamed asparagus
PointsPlus value per serving: 0

Game Plan

1. While oven preheats:
- Rinse and trim asparagus.

2. While fish cooks:
- Steam asparagus.
- Prepare cream sauce.
- Heat rice.

Menu
PointsPlus value
per serving: 9

Halibut with Quick Lemon
Pesto

Grilled Zucchini and Red Bell
Pepper with Corn

Game Plan

1. While grill heats:
- Wash and cut zucchini.
- Wash and cut bell
  pepper.

2. While vegetables and fish
cook:
- Prepare pesto.

3. Toss zucchini, bell pepper,
and corn with dressing,
salt, and black pepper.

Halibut with Quick Lemon Pesto

prep: 3 minutes • **cook:** 8 minutes   *PointsPlus* value per serving: 7

  4 (6-ounce) halibut or other firm white fish fillets
Cooking spray
  ¼ teaspoon salt, divided
  ⅛ teaspoon freshly ground black pepper
  ⅔ cup firmly packed basil leaves
  ¼ cup (1 ounce) grated fresh Parmesan cheese
  2 tablespoons extra-virgin olive oil
  2 garlic cloves, peeled
  1 tablespoon grated lemon rind
  1 tablespoon fresh lemon juice

1. Prepare grill.
2. Place fillets on grill rack coated with cooking spray. Sprinkle fish evenly with ⅛ teaspoon salt and pepper. Cover and grill 4 minutes on each side or until desired degree of doneness.
3. While fish grills, combine remaining ⅛ teaspoon salt, basil, and next 5 ingredients in a blender or food processor. Process until finely minced. Serve pesto over grilled fish. **Yield:** 4 servings (serving size: 1 fillet and about 1 tablespoon pesto).

Per serving: CALORIES 283; FAT 13g (sat 2.6g, mono 6.3g, poly 2.3g); PROTEIN 38.7g; CARB 1.4g; FIBER 0.5g; CHOL 59mg; IRON 1.7mg; SODIUM 363mg; CALC 195mg

Grilled Zucchini and Red Bell Pepper with Corn

prep: 5 minutes • **cook:** 10 minutes   *PointsPlus* value per serving: 2

  1 medium zucchini, halved lengthwise
  1 red bell pepper, halved lengthwise and seeded
Cooking spray
  1 cup frozen whole-kernel corn, thawed and drained
 1½ tablespoons Parmesan and roasted garlic salad dressing (such as Newman's Own)
  ¼ teaspoon salt
  ⅛ teaspoon crushed red pepper

1. Prepare grill.
2. Coat zucchini and bell pepper halves with cooking spray; place on grill rack. Cover and grill 5 minutes on each side or until bell pepper is charred and zucchini is tender.
3. Remove vegetables from grill; cut into 1-inch pieces. Place in a medium bowl. Stir in corn and remaining ingredients, tossing gently to combine. **Yield:** 4 servings (serving size: about ½ cup).

Per serving: CALORIES 74; FAT 3g (sat 0.5g, mono 0.1g, poly 0.2g); PROTEIN 2.3g; CARB 12.9g; FIBER 2.3g; CHOL 0mg; IRON 0.6mg; SODIUM 217mg; CALC 11mg

pictured on page 36

Chili-Garlic Glazed Salmon

prep: 4 minutes • **cook:** 7 minutes   *PointsPlus* value per serving: 7

The sweet, salty, and spicy flavors of this colorful glaze permeate the salmon as it cooks, creating a succulent dish that tantalizes the taste buds.

   3 tablespoons chili sauce with garlic (such as Hokan)
   3 tablespoons minced green onions (about 3 green onions)
1½ tablespoons low-sugar orange marmalade
   ¾ teaspoon lower-sodium soy sauce
   4 (6-ounce) salmon fillets
      Cooking spray

1. Preheat broiler.
2. Combine first 4 ingredients in a small bowl; brush half of chili sauce mixture over fillets. Place fillets, skin sides down, on a baking sheet coated with cooking spray. Broil fish 5 minutes; brush with remaining chili sauce mixture. Broil an additional 2 minutes or until desired degree of doneness. **Yield:** 4 servings (serving size: 1 fillet).

Per serving: CALORIES 298; FAT 13g (sat 3.1g, mono 5.7g, poly 3.2g); PROTEIN 36.3g; CARB 5.6g; FIBER 0.5g; CHOL 87mg; IRON 0.6mg; SODIUM 171mg; CALC 23mg

Minted Sugar Snap Peas

prep: 2 minutes • **cook:** 3 minutes   *PointsPlus* value per serving: 1

   1 teaspoon canola oil
   1 (8-ounce) package fresh sugar snap peas
   1 tablespoon chopped fresh mint
   1 teaspoon grated orange rind
   ¼ teaspoon salt

1. Heat oil in a large nonstick skillet over medium-high heat; add peas. Sauté 2 minutes or just until peas are crisp-tender. Stir in mint, orange rind, and salt. **Yield:** 4 servings (serving size: ½ cup).

Per serving: CALORIES 38; FAT 1g (sat 0.1g, mono 0.7g, poly 0.4g); PROTEIN 1.4g; CARB 4.9g; FIBER 1.4g; CHOL 0mg; IRON 0.8mg; SODIUM 152mg; CALC 42mg

---

Menu
PointsPlus value per serving: 8

Chili-Garlic Glazed Salmon

Minted Sugar Snap Peas

Game Plan

1. While broiler preheats:
 • Rinse and chop mint.
 • Grate orange rind.
 • Wash and mince green onions.

2. While fish cooks:
 • Prepare Minted Sugar Snap Peas.

Menu

PointsPlus value
per serving: 6

Lemon Red Snapper with Herbed Butter

Sautéed Zucchini and Bell Peppers

Game Plan

1. While oven preheats:
- Cut lemon; grate rind.
- Rinse and chop herbs.
- Wash and cut zucchini.
- Mince garlic.

2. While fish cooks:
- Prepare herbed butter.
- Prepare zucchini and peppers.

Lemon Red Snapper with Herbed Butter

prep: 9 minutes • **cook:** 13 minutes   *PointsPlus* value per serving: 5

A fragrant herbed butter and roasted lemon slices complement the sweet, nutty flavor of red snapper for a superfresh dish. Complete the meal with colorful Sautéed Zucchini and Bell Peppers.

　2　lemons
　　Cooking spray
　4　(6-ounce) red snapper or other firm white fish fillets
　¼　teaspoon salt
　¼　teaspoon paprika
　¼　teaspoon black pepper
　2　tablespoons butter, softened
1½　teaspoons chopped fresh herbs (such as rosemary, thyme, basil, or parsley)
　　Herb sprigs (optional)

1. Preheat oven to 425°.

2. Cut 1 lemon into 8 slices. Place slices, in pairs, on a rimmed baking sheet coated with cooking spray. Grate 1 teaspoon rind from remaining lemon; set aside. Reserve remaining lemon for another use.

3. Place 1 fillet on top of each pair of lemon slices. Combine salt, paprika, and pepper; sprinkle evenly over fish. Bake at 425° for 13 minutes or until desired degree of doneness.

4. While fish bakes, combine reserved lemon rind, butter, and herbs in a small bowl.

5. Place 1 fillet and 2 lemon slices on each of 4 plates; top each fillet with herbed butter, spreading to melt, if desired. Garnish with herb sprigs, if desired. **Yield:** 4 servings (serving size: 1 fillet and about 1½ teaspoons herbed butter).

Per serving: CALORIES 223; FAT 8g (sat 4.1g, mono 1.9g, poly 1g); PROTEIN 34g; CARB 2.9g; FIBER 0.9g; CHOL 75mg; IRON 0.5mg; SODIUM 259mg; CALC 62mg

Sautéed Zucchini and Bell Peppers

prep: 3 minutes • **cook:** 7 minutes   *PointsPlus* value per serving: 1

　1　teaspoon olive oil
　1　medium zucchini, quartered lengthwise and cut into 2-inch pieces
　1　cup refrigerated prechopped tricolor bell pepper
　¼　teaspoon salt
　1　garlic clove, minced

1. Heat oil in a large nonstick skillet over medium-high heat. Add zucchini and remaining ingredients; sauté 7 minutes. **Yield:** 4 servings (serving size: ½ cup).

Per serving: CALORIES 28; FAT 1g (sat 0.2g, mono 0.8g, poly 0.2g); PROTEIN 1.1g; CARB 3.9g; FIBER 0.8g; CHOL 0mg; IRON 0.4mg; SODIUM 148mg; CALC 14mg

Pan-Seared Snapper with Fennel-Olive Topping

prep: 6 minutes • **cook:** 13 minutes

PointsPlus value per serving: 6

Fennel bulb, when eaten raw in salads, has a subtle licorice flavor and crisp texture. When cooked, it mellows and softens. In this recipe, the sautéed fennel combines with the piquant tapenade to create a saucy and savory vegetable topping for the fish. Serve over rice.

 4 (6-ounce) red snapper or other firm white fish fillets
 ½ teaspoon salt
 ¼ teaspoon freshly ground black pepper
Cooking spray
 1 fennel bulb, thinly sliced (about 3½ cups)
 ½ cup thinly sliced onion
 1 large tomato, chopped
 3 tablespoons refrigerated olive tapenade
 2 tablespoons fresh lemon juice

1. Sprinkle fillets evenly with salt and pepper. Heat a large nonstick skillet over medium-high heat; coat pan and fillets with cooking spray. Add fish to pan, skin sides up. Cook 3 minutes or until lightly browned. Remove from pan.

2. Coat pan with cooking spray. Add fennel and onion; sauté 3 minutes. Add tomato, tapenade, and lemon juice; stir well. Return fillets to pan, nestling them into fennel mixture. Cover and cook 7 minutes or until desired degree of doneness. Spoon fennel mixture over fillets. **Yield:** 4 servings (serving size: 1 fillet and ¾ cup fennel topping).

Per serving: CALORIES 238; FAT 6g (sat 1.3g, mono 0.4g, poly 0.8g); PROTEIN 37g; CARB 8.9g; FIBER 3.4g; CHOL 63mg; IRON 1.4mg; SODIUM 545mg; CALC 107mg

Menu
PointsPlus value per serving: 9

Pan-Seared Snapper with Fennel-Olive Topping

½ cup precooked brown rice
PointsPlus value per serving: 3

Game Plan

1. Slice and wash fennel bulb.

2. Chop onion and tomato.

3. Prepare fish and fennel-olive topping.

4. Heat rice.

Menu
PointsPlus value
per serving: 10

Spicy Louisiana Tilapia Fillets
with Sautéed Vegetable Relish

Hoppin' John–Style Rice

Game Plan

1. Chop thyme and green
onions; mince garlic.

2. Prepare vegetable relish.

3. While fish cooks:
  • Sauté onions, garlic, and
    peas.
  • Microwave rice.
  • Assemble Hoppin' John–
    Style Rice.

4. Prepare butter mixture.

Spicy Louisiana Tilapia Fillets with Sautéed Vegetable Relish

prep: 5 minutes • **cook:** 10 minutes   *PointsPlus* value per serving: 5

Cooking spray
1   (8-ounce) container refrigerated prechopped tomato, onion, and bell pepper
    mix
4   (6-ounce) tilapia fillets
2   tablespoons water
2   teaspoons Louisiana hot sauce
1½ teaspoons chopped fresh thyme
½   teaspoon salt
1   tablespoon butter

1. Heat a large nonstick skillet over medium-high heat. Coat pan with cooking spray. Add tomato mixture; sauté 2 minutes. Remove from pan.
2. Coat pan and fillets with cooking spray; add fish to pan. Cook 2 minutes or until lightly browned. Turn fillets over; add tomato mixture to pan, spooning mixture over and around fillets. Cover and cook 5 minutes or until desired degree of doneness.
3. While fish cooks, combine 2 tablespoons water, hot sauce, thyme, and salt in a small bowl.
4. Carefully remove fish and tomato mixture from pan; place on a serving platter. Reduce heat to medium; add hot sauce mixture and butter to pan. Cook until butter melts. Spoon butter mixture evenly over fish and tomato mixture. **Yield:** 4 servings (serving size: 1 fillet and about ¼ cup tomato mixture).

Per serving: CALORIES 210; FAT 6g (sat 2.8g, mono 1.6g, poly 0.8g); PROTEIN 35g; CARB 4.8g; FIBER 1.4g; CHOL 93mg; IRON 1.4mg; SODIUM 465mg; CALC 34mg

Hoppin' John–Style Rice

prep: 4 minutes • **cook:** 4 minutes   *PointsPlus* value per serving: 5

2   teaspoons olive oil
¼   cup finely chopped green onions
1   garlic clove, minced
1   (15.8-ounce) can black-eyed peas, rinsed and drained
1   (8.8-ounce) pouch microwaveable cooked brown rice (such as Uncle Ben's
    Ready Rice)

1. Heat oil in a large nonstick skillet over medium-high heat; add onions and garlic. Sauté 30 seconds or until lightly browned. Add peas; cook 2 minutes or until thoroughly heated.
2. While peas cook, microwave rice according to package directions.
3. Add rice to pea mixture; toss well. **Yield:** 4 servings (serving size: ¾ cup).

Per serving: CALORIES 176; FAT 5g (sat 0.7g, mono 1.7g, poly 0.5g); PROTEIN 5.8g; CARB 28.6g; FIBER 3.4g; CHOL 0mg; IRON 1.1mg; SODIUM 131mg; CALC 20mg

pictured on page 35

Tilapia with Warm Olive Salsa

prep: 3 minutes • **cook:** 9 minutes   *PointsPlus* value per serving: 5

Cooking spray
1 cup chopped plum tomato (about ⅓ pound)
12 small pimiento-stuffed olives, chopped
2 tablespoons chopped fresh parsley
1½ teaspoons chopped fresh oregano, divided
4 (6-ounce) tilapia fillets, rinsed and patted dry
¼ teaspoon salt
¼ teaspoon freshly ground black pepper
4 lemon wedges
1 tablespoon extra-virgin olive oil

1. Heat a large nonstick skillet over medium-high heat. Coat pan with cooking spray. Add tomato; cook 1 minute or until thoroughly heated. Combine cooked tomato, olives, parsley, and ¾ teaspoon oregano in a small bowl; keep warm.
2. Wipe pan dry with a paper towel; return pan to medium-high heat. Recoat pan with cooking spray. Sprinkle fillets evenly with remaining ¾ teaspoon oregano, salt, and pepper. Add fillets to pan; cook 3 minutes on each side or until desired degree of doneness. Squeeze 1 lemon wedge over each fillet; drizzle evenly with oil. Top evenly with olive salsa. **Yield:** 4 servings (serving size: 1 fillet and ¼ cup olive salsa).

Per serving: CALORIES 218; FAT 8g (sat 1.7g, mono 4.5g, poly 1.1g); PROTEIN 34.8g; CARB 3.1g; FIBER 1g; CHOL 85mg; IRON 1.4mg; SODIUM 485mg; CALC 36mg

Lemon Couscous with Toasted Pine Nuts

prep: 3 minutes • **cook:** 5 minutes • **other:** 5 minutes
PointsPlus value per serving: 4

1 cup water
⅔ cup uncooked whole-wheat couscous
1 teaspoon grated lemon rind
¼ cup pine nuts, toasted
2 teaspoons extra-virgin olive oil
¼ teaspoon salt

1. Bring 1 cup water to a boil in a small saucepan. Stir in couscous and lemon rind. Remove from heat; cover and let stand 5 minutes. Add pine nuts and remaining ingredients; fluff with a fork. **Yield:** 4 servings (serving size: about ½ cup).

Per serving: CALORIES 148; FAT 8g (sat 0.7g, mono 3.4g, poly 3.1g); PROTEIN 3.8g; CARB 16.2g; FIBER 2.7g; CHOL 0mg; IRON 1.1mg; SODIUM 146mg; CALC 9mg

---

Menu
PointsPlus value per serving: 9

Tilapia with Warm Olive Salsa

Lemon Couscous with Toasted Pine Nuts

Game Plan

1. While water for couscous comes to a boil:
• Toast pine nuts.
• Wash and chop plum tomatoes and parsley.
• Grate lemon rind.

2. While fish cooks:
• Prepare couscous.

3. Top cooked fish with lemon juice, olive oil, and olive salsa.

Menu

PointsPlus value
per serving: 15

Pan-Seared Tarragon Trout

**Fig, Carrot, and Ginger
Rice Pilaf**

Game Plan

1. Grate lemon rind, and juice lemon.

2. Mince ginger and garlic.

3. While fish cooks:
- Cook rice and carrots, ginger, and garlic.
- Assemble Rice Pilaf; keep warm.

4. Prepare garlic sauce for fish.

Pan-Seared Tarragon Trout

prep: 7 minutes • **cook:** 8 minutes   *PointsPlus* value per serving: 9

1   lemon
2   tablespoons all-purpose flour
2   (6-ounce) trout fillets
¼   teaspoon salt
¼   teaspoon freshly ground black pepper
1   tablespoon butter
1   garlic clove, minced
¼   cup dry white wine
1   teaspoon dried tarragon

1. Grate ¼ teaspoon rind from lemon; squeeze juice to measure 1 teaspoon. Set aside.
2. Place flour in a shallow dish. Sprinkle fish evenly with salt and pepper; dredge fish in flour.
3. Melt butter in a large nonstick skillet over medium-high heat. Add fish; cook 2 to 3 minutes on each side or until desired degree of doneness. Remove fish from pan; keep warm.
4. Add garlic to pan; sauté 1 minute or until browned. Add wine; cook until liquid almost evaporates, scraping pan to loosen browned bits. Stir in tarragon and reserved lemon rind and juice. Pour garlic sauce over fish. **Yield:** 2 servings (serving size: 1 fillet and about 1 tablespoon sauce).

Per serving: CALORIES 293; FAT 12g (sat 4.8g, mono 3.4g, poly 2.4g); PROTEIN 36g; CARB 6.2g; FIBER 0.4g; CHOL 115mg; IRON 1.8mg; SODIUM 385mg; CALC 133mg

Fig, Carrot, and Ginger Rice Pilaf

prep: 4 minutes • **cook:** 5 minutes   *PointsPlus* value per serving: 6

1   (8.8-ounce) pouch microwaveable cooked brown rice (such as Uncle Ben's Ready Rice)
1   tablespoon olive oil
1   cup matchstick-cut carrots
1   tablespoon minced peeled fresh ginger
2   garlic cloves, minced
½   cup small dried figs, quartered

1. Heat rice according to package directions; keep warm.
2. While rice cooks, heat oil in a large nonstick skillet over medium-high heat; add carrots, ginger, and garlic. Sauté 3 minutes or until browned. Add figs; sauté 2 minutes or until hot. Remove from heat; stir in rice. Serve immediately. **Yield:** 4 servings (serving size: about ½ cup).

Per serving: CALORIES 217; FAT 6g (sat 0.8g, mono 2.6g, poly 0.6g); PROTEIN 3.7g; CARB 39.8g; FIBER 4.3g; CHOL 0mg; IRON 1mg; SODIUM 24mg; CALC 52mg

pictured on page 37

Seared Sesame Tuna with Orange-Ginger Sauce

prep: 7 minutes • **cook:** 7 minutes   *PointsPlus* value per serving: 8

 3 tablespoons orange-ginger sauce and glaze (such as Iron Chef)
 1 tablespoon seasoned rice vinegar
 1 teaspoon lower-sodium soy sauce
 ½ teaspoon dark sesame oil
 1 garlic clove, minced
 2 teaspoons canola oil
 4 (6-ounce) tuna steaks (about 1 inch thick)
 ⅛ teaspoon salt
 3 tablespoons sesame seeds
 3 tablespoons black sesame seeds
    Cooking spray
 ¼ cup sliced green onions

1. Combine first 5 ingredients, stirring well with a whisk; set aside.

2. Heat canola oil in a large nonstick skillet over medium-high heat. Sprinkle steaks evenly with salt. Combine sesame seeds and black sesame seeds in a shallow dish. Dredge steaks in sesame seeds. Lightly coat both sides of fish with cooking spray. Add fish to pan; cook 3 minutes on each side or until desired degree of doneness. Sprinkle evenly with onions; serve with orange-ginger sauce. **Yield:** 4 servings (serving size: 1 steak and 1½ tablespoons sauce).

Per serving: CALORIES 317; FAT 11g (sat 1.6g, mono 4.2g, poly 4.1g); PROTEIN 42.3g; CARB 10.4g; FIBER 1.9g; CHOL 77mg; IRON 3.3mg; SODIUM 302mg; CALC 165mg

---

Menu
PointsPlus value per serving: 12

Seared Sesame Tuna with Orange-Ginger Sauce

Edamame and Corn Salad

Game Plan

1. Measure and combine ingredients for salad.

2. Prepare coating for fish.

3. While fish cooks:
 • Toss salad.

Edamame and Corn Salad

prep: 7 minutes   *PointsPlus* value per serving: 4

 ¼ cup seasoned rice vinegar
 2 tablespoons water
 1 tablespoon olive oil
 1 teaspoon brown sugar
 1 teaspoon minced peeled fresh ginger
 ⅛ teaspoon salt
 1 (10-ounce) package refrigerated shelled edamame (green soybeans)
 1 cup frozen whole-kernel corn, thawed and drained
 1 tablespoon chopped fresh cilantro

1. Combine first 6 ingredients in a medium bowl, stirring well with a whisk. Add edamame, corn, and cilantro; toss gently to coat. **Yield:** 4 servings (serving size: ⅔ cup).

Per serving: CALORIES 156; FAT 7g (sat 0.5g, mono 2.6g, poly 0.6g); PROTEIN 8.4g; CARB 17.7g; FIBER 4.3g; CHOL 0mg; IRON 1.7mg; SODIUM 376mg; CALC 45mg

Menu
PointsPlus value
per serving: 6

Spicy Thai Tuna Cakes with
Cucumber Aioli

Orange and Radish
Cabbage Slaw

Game Plan

1. Slice radishes, and section
orange for slaw.

2. Chop cilantro; prepare
patties.

3. While patties cook:
• Prepare cucumber aioli.
• Toss slaw mixture.

Spicy Thai Tuna Cakes with Cucumber Aioli

prep: 10 minutes • **cook:** 2 minutes   *PointsPlus* value per serving: 4

Cool cucumber aioli puts out the fire of the Thai spices in these tuna cakes. Although the cakes are portioned as a main dish, you can also form eight smaller appetizer cakes when entertaining guests.

    3 (5-ounce) cans Thai chili-flavored tuna (such as Bumble Bee), drained
    1 large egg white, lightly beaten
    ½ cup panko (Japanese breadcrumbs)
    2 tablespoons chopped fresh cilantro
    Cooking spray
    ½ cup shredded cucumber
    ¼ cup light mayonnaise

1. Combine first 4 ingredients in a medium bowl. Divide tuna mixture into 4 equal portions, shaping each into a ¾-inch-thick patty.
2. Heat a large nonstick skillet over medium heat. Coat pan and patties with cooking spray. Add patties; cook 1 to 2 minutes on each side or until lightly browned.
3. While patties cook, combine cucumber and mayonnaise in a small bowl. Serve with tuna cakes. **Yield:** 4 servings (serving size: 1 cake and 2 tablespoons aioli).

Per serving: CALORIES 173; FAT 9g (sat 1.2g, mono 3.8g, poly 3.6g); PROTEIN 10.1g; CARB 11.9g; FIBER 0.9g; CHOL 26mg; IRON 0.8mg; SODIUM 413mg; CALC 4mg

Orange and Radish Cabbage Slaw

prep: 6 minutes   *PointsPlus* value per serving: 2

    4 cups shredded napa (Chinese) cabbage
    ½ cup sliced radishes (about 3 radishes)
    ⅓ cup orange sections (about 1 small orange)
    2 tablespoons rice vinegar
    1 tablespoon canola oil
    2 teaspoons sugar
    1 teaspoon dark sesame oil

1. Combine first 3 ingredients in a large bowl.
2. Combine vinegar and next 3 ingredients in a small bowl, stirring well with a whisk. Pour vinegar mixture over cabbage mixture; toss gently to coat. **Yield:** 4 servings (serving size: 1¼ cups).

Per serving: CALORIES 76; FAT 5g (sat 0.4g, mono 2.1g, poly 1g); PROTEIN 1.2g; CARB 8g; FIBER 1.6g; CHOL 0mg; IRON 0mg; SODIUM 11mg; CALC 70mg

Fresh Garlic Linguine with Clams

prep: 3 minutes • **cook:** 8 minutes   *PointsPlus* value per serving: 10

Pay close attention to the clams when scrubbing them. If some are opened slightly, give them a gentle tap. If they close, they're fine; if they don't, discard them. If any clams remain closed after they have cooked, discard them as well.

1   (9-ounce) package refrigerated linguine or angel hair pasta
2   teaspoons olive oil
4   garlic cloves, minced
½   cup chopped bottled roasted red bell peppers
24 littleneck clams, scrubbed
¼   cup dry white wine
⅓   cup finely chopped fresh parsley, divided
¾   cup (3 ounces) grated Asiago cheese, divided

1. Cook pasta according to package directions, omitting salt and fat. Drain, reserving ¼ cup pasta water.
2. While pasta cooks, heat oil in a large nonstick skillet over medium-high heat. Add garlic and bell pepper. Cook 1 minute, stirring constantly. Add clams and wine. Cover and cook 3 to 4 minutes or until shells open.
3. Add pasta and half of parsley to clams in pan, tossing well to blend. Add reserved ¼ cup pasta water and half of cheese, tossing well to blend. Sprinkle remaining parsley and cheese evenly over each serving. **Yield:** 4 servings (serving size: 6 clams and 1 cup pasta).

Per serving: CALORIES 339g; FAT 11g (sat 4.9g, mono 3.3g, poly 0.7g); PROTEIN 20.8g; CARB 38.1g; FIBER 1.7g; CHOL 75mg; IRON 9.3mg; SODIUM 155mg; CALC 258mg

Menu
PointsPlus value per serving: 11

Fresh Garlic Linguine with Clams

½ cup steamed sugar snap peas
PointsPlus value per serving: 1

Game Plan

1. While water for pasta comes to a boil:
• Scrub clams.
• Mince garlic.
• Chop peppers and parsley.
• Grate cheese.

2. While pasta cooks:
• Cook garlic, bell pepper, clam, and wine mixture.

3. Add pasta to clam sauce, and add cheese.

4. Steam peas.

pictured on page 38

Scallops with Capers and Tomatoes

Menu
PointsPlus value
per serving: 8

Scallops with Capers and
Tomatoes

½ cup angel hair pasta
PointsPlus value
per serving: 3

Game Plan

1. While water for pasta
comes to a boil:
• Mince garlic.
• Seed and dice tomatoes.
• Chop basil.

2. While pasta cooks:
• Cook scallops.
• Prepare sauce.

prep: 5 minutes • **cook:** 7 minutes   *PointsPlus* value per serving: 5

Always request dry-packed sea scallops. They tend to be fresher and haven't been soaked in water to increase their weight. Serve these scallops over hot cooked angel hair pasta.

12 large sea scallops (about 1½ pounds)
  Cooking spray
 1 garlic clove, minced
 ½ cup dry white wine
 1 tomato, seeded and diced (about 1 cup)
 3 tablespoons capers, drained
 2 tablespoons chopped fresh basil
 ¼ teaspoon salt
 1 tablespoon extra-virgin olive oil

1. Pat scallops dry with paper towels. Heat a large nonstick skillet over medium-high heat. Coat pan with cooking spray. Add scallops to pan; cook 3 minutes on each side or until done. Remove scallops from pan; keep warm.
2. Add garlic to pan; cook 15 seconds. Add wine and next 4 ingredients to pan. Spoon mixture over scallops; drizzle evenly with oil just before serving. **Yield:** 4 servings (serving size: 3 scallops and ⅓ cup sauce).

Per serving: CALORIES 212; FAT 5g (sat 0.7g, mono 2.8g, poly 0.8g); PROTEIN 29.1g; CARB 6.8g; FIBER 0.7g; CHOL 56mg; IRON 0.8mg; SODIUM 614mg; CALC 53mg

Southwestern Breakfast Wraps | page 11

Pecan-Apple Sticky Buns | page 8

Tilapia with Warm Olive Salsa | page 27

Chili-Garlic Glazed Salmon | page 23

Seared Sesame Tuna with Orange-Ginger
Sauce | page 29

Scallops with Capers and Tomatoes | page 32

Shrimp with Creamy Orange-Chipotle Sauce | page 50

39

Grilled Heirloom Tomato and
Goat Cheese Pizza | page 58

Mushroom Stroganoff | page 63

41

Orange Beef and Broccoli | page 69

Mustard-Molasses Flank
Steak | page 70

Slow-Cooker Beef Pot Roast | page 72

Lemon-Herb Skillet Pork Chops | page 74

45

Sherried Pineapple Pork
Tenderloin | page 76

Balsamic Chicken with Roasted Tomatoes | page 89

47

Grilled Asian Drumsticks | page 94

Deep South Shrimp and Sausage

prep: 4 minutes • **cook:** 9 minutes • **other:** 2 minutes
PointsPlus value per serving: 3

Our lightened version of Lowcountry shrimp and grits is high on flavor and low in fat and calories.

Cooking spray
¾ pound peeled and deveined medium shrimp
1 teaspoon Old Bay seasoning
¼ teaspoon freshly ground black pepper
1 cup refrigerated prechopped tricolor bell pepper
1 (6.5-ounce) link smoked turkey sausage, cut into ⅛-inch-thick slices
2 garlic cloves, minced
¼ cup water

1. Heat a large nonstick skillet over medium-high heat. Coat pan with cooking spray. Add shrimp, seasoning, and black pepper, tossing to coat. Cook 3 minutes or until shrimp are done, stirring frequently. Remove from pan; keep warm.
2. Return pan to medium-high heat. Coat pan with cooking spray. Add bell pepper; cook 2 minutes, stirring frequently. Add sausage; cook 2 minutes or until lightly browned, stirring frequently. Add reserved shrimp mixture and garlic. Cook 1 minute, stirring constantly. Add ¼ cup water; cook 30 seconds, scraping pan to loosen browned bits. Remove from heat; let stand 2 minutes. **Yield:** 4 servings (serving size: ¾ cup).

Per serving: CALORIES 142; FAT 3g (sat 1g, mono 0.1g, poly 0.3g); PROTEIN 19.7g; CARB 7.6g; FIBER 0.6g; CHOL 147mg; IRON 2.8mg; SODIUM 701mg; CALC 48mg

Menu

PointsPlus value per serving: 6

Deep South Shrimp and Sausage

Spicy Cheese Grits

Game Plan

1. While water for grits comes to a boil:
  • Slice sausage.
  • Mince garlic.

2. While grits cook:
  • Cook shrimp, sausage, and bell pepper mixture.

Spicy Cheese Grits

prep: 3 minutes • **cook:** 7 minutes   *PointsPlus* value per serving: 3

1½ cups water
½ cup uncooked quick-cooking grits
½ cup fat-free milk
¼ cup (1 ounce) grated fresh Parmesan cheese
¼ teaspoon salt
¾ teaspoon hot sauce
¼ teaspoon Worcestershire sauce

1. Bring 1½ cups water to a boil in a medium saucepan. Gradually stir in grits. Cover, reduce heat, and simmer 5 minutes. Stir in milk. Remove from heat; add remaining ingredients, stirring until cheese melts. **Yield:** 4 servings (serving size: ½ cup).

Per serving: CALORIES 111; FAT 2g (sat 1.2g, mono 0.1g, poly 0.1g); PROTEIN 5.1g; CARB 17.5g; FIBER 0.3g; CHOL 7mg; IRON 0.8mg; SODIUM 275mg; CALC 113mg

pictured on page 39

Shrimp with Creamy Orange-Chipotle Sauce

prep: 3 minutes • **cook:** 6 minutes   *PointsPlus* value per serving: 4

The half-and-half and grated orange rind create a citrusy cream sauce that tames the spiciness of the chipotle chile. Serve with hot cooked linguine, if desired.

⅔   cup half-and-half
1   teaspoon grated orange rind
1   large chipotle chile, canned in adobo sauce
Cooking spray
1½   pounds peeled and deveined large shrimp
¾   teaspoon ground cumin
¼   teaspoon salt
2   tablespoons chopped fresh cilantro

1. Place first 3 ingredients in a blender; process until smooth.
2. Heat a large nonstick skillet over medium-high heat. Coat pan with cooking spray; add shrimp. Coat shrimp with cooking spray; sprinkle with cumin and salt. Sauté 4 minutes or until shrimp are done, stirring frequently. Transfer shrimp to a serving platter. Reduce heat to medium, add half-and-half mixture to pan, and cook 1 minute, stirring constantly. Pour sauce over shrimp; sprinkle with cilantro.
Yield: 4 servings (serving size: ½ cup shrimp and 2 tablespoons sauce).

Per serving: CALORIES 186; FAT 6g (sat 3.3g, mono 0.3g, poly 0.6g); PROTEIN 28.3g; CARB 2.6g; FIBER 0.5g; CHOL 267mg; IRON 4.3mg; SODIUM 494mg; CALC 97mg

Szechuan Shrimp

prep: 2 minutes • **cook:** 7 minutes   *PointsPlus* value per serving: 4

Similar in texture and flavor to peanuts, soy nuts add a nutty crunch to this Chinese classic. If you can't find soy nuts, substitute lightly salted or unsalted dry-roasted peanuts. Serve with rice and steamed broccoli.

    Cooking spray
1½ pounds peeled and deveined large shrimp
¾   teaspoon crushed red pepper
½   cup light sesame-ginger dressing (such as Newman's Own)
4   green onions, cut into 1-inch pieces
2   tablespoons lightly salted soy nuts, toasted and coarsely chopped

1. Heat a large nonstick skillet over medium-high heat. Coat pan with cooking spray. Coat shrimp with cooking spray; add shrimp and red pepper to pan. Stir-fry 2 minutes. Add dressing and onions. Cook 3 minutes or until shrimp are done, stirring constantly. Sprinkle evenly with soy nuts; serve immediately. **Yield:** 4 servings (serving size: 1 cup).

Per serving: CALORIES 190; FAT 4g (sat 0.6g, mono 0.3g, poly 0.6g); PROTEIN 29.5g; CARB 7.9g; FIBER 1.4g; CHOL 252mg; IRON 4.4mg; SODIUM 708mg; CALC 72mg

---

Menu
PointsPlus value
per serving: 7

Szechuan Shrimp

½ cup precooked brown rice
PointsPlus value
per serving: 3

1 cup steamed broccoli
PointsPlus value
per serving: 0

Game Plan

1. While broccoli cooks:
• Toast and chop soy nuts.
• Chop green onions.

2. Prepare shrimp.

3. Heat rice.

Menu

PointsPlus value
per serving: 6

Chili-Lime Shrimp

1 slice whole-wheat
French bread
PointsPlus value
per serving: 2

½ cup sautéed green beans
PointsPlus value
per serving: 0

Game Plan

1. Chop onions.

2. Juice lime.

3. While onions and shrimp
   cook:
   • Sauté green beans
     with cooking spray and
     parsley.

Chili-Lime Shrimp

prep: 4 minutes • **cook:** 6 minutes   *PointsPlus* value per serving: 4

The bright, tart flavor of freshly squeezed lime juice balances the heat of the chili powder in the rich sauce that coats these shrimp. Serve with crusty whole-wheat French bread to soak up the sauce.

Cooking spray
¾   cup chopped green onions, divided
1½ pounds peeled and deveined large shrimp
1   teaspoon chili powder
2   tablespoons fresh lime juice (about 1 lime)
2   tablespoons butter
½   teaspoon salt

1. Heat a large nonstick skillet over medium-high heat. Coat pan with cooking spray. Add ½ cup onions; coat onions with cooking spray. Cook 1 minute, stirring occasionally. Add shrimp and chili powder; cook 4 minutes or until desired degree of doneness, stirring occasionally. Remove from heat. Add lime juice, butter, and salt, and stir until butter melts. Sprinkle with remaining ¼ cup onions. **Yield:** 4 servings (serving size: 1 cup).

Per serving: CALORIES 186; FAT 7g (sat 4g, mono 1.7g, poly 0.8g); PROTEIN 27.5g; CARB 2g; FIBER 0.5g; CHOL 267mg; IRON 4.3mg; SODIUM 644mg; CALC 67mg

Broiled Shrimp Kebabs with Horseradish-Herb Sour Cream Sauce

prep: 9 minutes • **cook:** 4 minutes   *PointsPlus* value per serving: 5

The warm, juicy cherry tomatoes offer a hint of acidity and a pleasing contrast to the shrimp. Soak the wooden skewers in water at least 30 minutes prior to broiling so they don't burn.

40   large shrimp, peeled and deveined with tails intact (about 1½ pounds)
16   cherry tomatoes
 Olive oil–flavored cooking spray
 2   teaspoons salt-free steak seasoning (such as Mrs. Dash)
¼   teaspoon salt
 Lemon wedges
 Horseradish-Herb Sour Cream Sauce

1. Preheat broiler.
2. Place shrimp and tomatoes in a large bowl; coat with cooking spray. Sprinkle evenly with steak seasoning and salt, tossing to coat. Thread 5 shrimp and 2 tomatoes onto each of 8 (10-inch) wooden skewers.
3. Place kebabs on a foil-lined baking sheet coated with cooking spray. Broil 4 to 5 minutes or until shrimp are done, turning once. Serve with lemon wedges and Horseradish-Herb Sour Cream Sauce. **Yield:** 4 servings (serving size: 2 skewers and 2 tablespoons sauce).

Per serving: CALORIES 205; FAT 8g (sat 2.2g, mono 1.9g, poly 0.9g); PROTEIN 26.2g; CARB 6.8g; FIBER 0.9g; CHOL 241mg; IRON 3.9mg; SODIUM 675mg; CALC 55mg

Horseradish-Herb Sour Cream Sauce

prep: 3 minutes   *PointsPlus* value per serving: 1

⅓   cup light sour cream
 2   tablespoons light mayonnaise
 1   teaspoon chopped fresh rosemary
 2   teaspoons extra-virgin olive oil
 1   teaspoon prepared horseradish
 1   teaspoon Dijon mustard
¼   teaspoon salt

1. Combine all ingredients in a small bowl, stirring until well blended. **Yield:** ½ cup (serving size: 1 tablespoon).

Per serving: CALORIES 36; FAT 3g (sat 0.9g, mono 0.9g, poly 0.1g); PROTEIN 0.3g; CARB 1.8g; FIBER 0g; CHOL 5mg; IRON 0mg; SODIUM 130mg; CALC 1mg

---

Menu
PointsPlus value per serving: 8

Broiled Shrimp Kebabs with Horseradish-Herb Sour Cream Sauce

½ cup sautéed spinach
PointsPlus value per serving: 0

½ cup microwave potatoes
PointsPlus value per serving: 3

Game Plan

1. While broiler preheats:
   • Assemble kebabs.
   • Prepare Sour Cream Sauce.

2. While kebabs cook:
   • Sauté spinach with cooking spray and herbs.
   • Prepare potatoes.

Game Plan

1. While water for pasta
   comes to a boil:
   • Chop oregano.

2. While pasta and shrimp
   cook:
   • Prepare cheese sauce for
   shrimp.

Creamy Garlic Shrimp and Pasta

prep: 2 minutes • **cook:** 9 minutes   *PointsPlus* value per serving: 10

3   quarts water
1   (9-ounce) package fresh linguine
1   pound peeled and deveined large shrimp
½   cup fat-free milk
⅓   cup plus 1½ tablespoons (3 ounces) light garlic-and-herbs spreadable cheese
     (such as Alouette Light)
¼   cup dry white wine
½   teaspoon salt
3   garlic cloves, pressed
1½   tablespoons chopped fresh oregano
     Oregano sprigs (optional)

1. Bring 3 quarts water to a boil in a large Dutch oven; add pasta and shrimp. Cook 3 to 4 minutes or until pasta is tender and shrimp are done. Drain and keep warm.
2. While pasta and shrimp cook, combine milk and next 4 ingredients in a large nonstick skillet over medium-high heat. Bring to a boil. Reduce heat; simmer 2 minutes or until slightly thick, stirring constantly.
3. Add pasta and shrimp to sauce in pan, tossing to coat. Stir in chopped oregano just before serving. Garnish with oregano sprigs, if desired. **Yield:** 4 servings (serving size: 1¼ cups).

Per serving: CALORIES 337; FAT 7g (sat 3.3g, mono 0.2g, poly 0.4g); PROTEIN 28.7g; CARB 38.4g; FIBER 1.6g; CHOL 220mg; IRON 4.1mg; SODIUM 571mg; CALC 116mg

Meatless Main Dishes

Menu

PointsPlus value per serving: 9

Refried Bean Poblanos with Cheese

Creamy Chipotle Wedge Salad

Game Plan

1. Halve and seed poblanos.

2. While poblanos are in microwave:
   • Combine rice, beans, and picante sauce.

3. Assemble poblanos.

4. While poblanos and rice mixture cook:
   • Blend dressing, onions, and chipotle chile.

5. While cheese melts:
   • Assemble salad.

Refried Bean Poblanos with Cheese

prep: 2 minutes • **cook:** 6 minutes   *PointsPlus* value per serving: 7

Poblano chiles grown in a hot, dry climate can be more intense than others, so the spiciness of this dish depends on the heat of your peppers.

4   medium poblano chiles, halved and seeded
1   (16-ounce) can fat-free refried beans
1   (8.8-ounce) pouch microwaveable cooked long-grain rice (such as Uncle Ben's Original Ready Rice)
½   cup picante sauce
1   cup (4 ounces) preshredded reduced-fat 4-cheese Mexican blend cheese
Chopped fresh cilantro (optional)

1. Place chile halves, cut sides up, on a round microwave-safe plate. Cover with wax paper; microwave at HIGH 3 minutes.

2. While chiles cook, combine beans, rice, and picante sauce in a medium bowl, stirring well. Spoon bean mixture evenly into chile halves. Cover with wax paper; microwave at HIGH 2 minutes. Uncover chiles, sprinkle each half with 2 tablespoons cheese, and microwave at HIGH 1 to 2 minutes or until cheese melts. Sprinkle evenly with cilantro, if desired. **Yield:** 4 servings (serving size: 2 stuffed chile halves).

Per serving: CALORIES 303; FAT 6g (sat 3.1g, mono 0g, poly 0.1g); PROTEIN 17g; CARB 45.4g; FIBER 7.7g; CHOL 10mg; IRON 0.7mg; SODIUM 960mg; CALC 232mg

Creamy Chipotle Wedge Salad

prep: 5 minutes   *PointsPlus* value per serving: 2

½   cup light ranch dressing (such as Naturally Fresh)
1   chipotle chile, canned in adobo sauce
1   green onion, cut into 2-inch pieces
½   head iceberg lettuce, cored and quartered

1. Place first 3 ingredients in a blender; process until smooth. Serve over lettuce wedges. **Yield:** 4 servings (serving size: 1 lettuce wedge and 2½ tablespoons dressing).

Per serving: CALORIES 90; FAT 7g (sat 0.6g, mono 1.2g, poly 5.1g); PROTEIN 1g; CARB 5.8g; FIBER 1.2g; CHOL 8mg; IRON 0.5mg; SODIUM 338mg; CALC 23mg

Grilled Polenta with Tomatoes and White Beans

prep: 5 minutes • **cook:** 10 minutes   *PointsPlus* value per serving: 8

The tomato-and–white bean mixture and the polenta cook in only a matter of minutes. To keep this recipe quick and easy yet deliver attractive grill marks, we used a grill pan instead of firing up an outdoor grill. If you don't have a grill pan, use a nonstick skillet.

  1   (17-ounce) tube of basil and garlic–flavored polenta, cut into 9 slices
Cooking spray
  2   teaspoons olive oil
  2   cups halved grape tomatoes
  2   garlic cloves, minced
  1   (15-ounce) can cannellini beans, rinsed and drained
  1   tablespoon white wine vinegar
1½   teaspoons chopped fresh rosemary
  ¼   teaspoon freshly ground black pepper
  ½   cup (2 ounces) grated Parmigiano-Reggiano cheese
Rosemary sprigs (optional)

1. Heat a grill pan or nonstick skillet over medium-high heat. Coat pan and polenta slices with cooking spray. Place polenta slices on pan; cook 2 minutes on each side or until golden brown. Remove from pan; keep warm.

2. While polenta cooks, heat oil in a large nonstick skillet over medium-high heat. Add tomatoes and garlic to pan; sauté 4 minutes or until tomatoes soften and garlic is tender. Reduce heat to low. Stir in beans and next 3 ingredients. Cook, stirring constantly, 2 minutes or until thoroughly heated.

3. Place 3 polenta slices on each of 3 plates. Spoon tomato mixture evenly over polenta, and sprinkle evenly with cheese. Garnish with rosemary sprigs, if desired. **Yield:** 3 servings (serving size: 3 polenta slices, 1 cup tomato mixture, and about 2½ tablespoons cheese).

Per serving: CALORIES 331; FAT 9g (sat 4.2g, mono 2.7g, poly 1.6g); PROTEIN 13.8g; CARB 43.5g; FIBER 5.7g; CHOL 19mg; IRON 2.2mg; SODIUM 993mg; CALC 296mg

Menu
PointsPlus value
per serving: 8

Grilled Polenta with Tomatoes and White Beans

1 cup grilled zucchini
PointsPlus value
per serving: 0

Game Plan

1. While grill heats:
  • Slice polenta.
  • Drain and rinse beans.

2. While polenta cooks:
  • Sauté tomatoes, garlic, and beans.

3. Grill zucchini.

pictured on page 40

Grilled Heirloom Tomato and Goat Cheese Pizza

prep: 11 minutes • **cook:** 4 minutes   *PointsPlus* value per serving: 7

Menu
PointsPlus value
per serving: 14

Grilled Heirloom Tomato and
Goat Cheese Pizza

1 cup mixed greens with
fat-free vinaigrette
PointsPlus value per
serving: 0

Peanut Butter–Chocolate
Banana Split

Game Plan

1. While grill heats:
 • Seed and chop tomato.
 • Assemble pizza.

2. While pizza cooks:
 • Toss salad.

3. Prepare Peanut Butter–
Chocolate Banana Split.

Heirloom tomatoes are remarkably flavorful and colorful compared to their grocery store counterparts. Variations include red, orange, gold, taxi yellow, nearly white, pink, purplish black, and green. Some are even multicolored, such as Mr. Stripey, which we used here. Your choice of tomato will shine in this simple pizza.

   1   (13.8-ounce) can refrigerated pizza crust dough
       Cooking spray
   1   garlic clove, halved
   1   large heirloom tomato, seeded and chopped (about 10 ounces)
   ¾   cup (3 ounces) crumbled herbed goat cheese
   ½   cup (2 ounces) shredded part-skim mozzarella cheese

1. Prepare grill.
2. Unroll dough onto a large baking sheet coated with cooking spray; pat dough into a 12 x 9–inch rectangle. Lightly coat dough with cooking spray.
3. Place dough on grill rack coated with cooking spray; grill 1 minute or until lightly browned. Turn crust over. Rub with garlic; sprinkle with tomato and cheeses. Close grill lid; grill 3 minutes. Serve immediately. **Yield:** 6 servings (serving size: 1 slice).

Per serving: CALORIES 242; FAT 8g (sat 4.4g, mono 1.4g, poly 0.2g); PROTEIN 10.7g; CARB 33.1g; FIBER 0.4g; CHOL 17mg; IRON 2.2mg; SODIUM 590mg; CALC 107mg

Peanut Butter–Chocolate Banana Split

prep: 7 minutes • **cook:** 1 minute   *PointsPlus* value per serving: 7

   ¼   cup plus 2 tablespoons chocolate syrup
   1½ tablespoons reduced-fat peanut butter
   3   bananas, cut in half lengthwise
   3   cups vanilla bean light ice cream (such as Edy's)
   3   tablespoons chopped unsalted peanuts

1. Combine chocolate syrup and peanut butter in a 1-cup glass measure. Microwave at HIGH 40 seconds or until peanut butter melts. Stir until smooth.
2. Cut each banana half crosswise into 2 pieces. Arrange 2 banana pieces in each of 6 dessert dishes; top banana with ice cream and hot chocolate sauce. Sprinkle with peanuts. Serve immediately. **Yield:** 6 servings (serving size: 2 pieces banana, ½ cup ice cream, about 1½ tablespoons chocolate sauce, and 1½ teaspoons peanuts).

Per serving: CALORIES 255; FAT 7g (sat 2.6g, mono 1.1g, poly 0.7g); PROTEIN 6g; CARB 44.9g; FIBER 2.1g; CHOL 20mg; IRON 0.6mg; SODIUM 82mg; CALC 62mg

Spaghetti with Zucchini and White Beans

prep: 5 minutes • **cook:** 10 minutes   *PointsPlus* value per serving: 8

Tender spaghetti noodles capture the fresh taste of the chunky bean and vegetable sauce, while feta cheese adds a finishing touch.

    6   ounces uncooked spaghetti
        Olive oil–flavored cooking spray
    3   cups (¼-inch) diced zucchini (2 medium)
    ⅓   cup water
    1   tablespoon tomato paste (such as Amore)
    ¼   teaspoon kosher salt
    ⅛   teaspoon coarsely ground black pepper
    1   (15.8-ounce) can Great Northern beans, rinsed and drained
    1   (14.5-ounce) can diced tomatoes with basil, garlic, and oregano, undrained
    ½   cup (2 ounces) crumbled feta cheese

1. Cook spaghetti according to package directions, omitting salt and fat.

2. While pasta cooks, heat a large nonstick skillet over medium-high heat. Coat pan with cooking spray. Add zucchini to pan; cook 5 minutes or until lightly browned, stirring occasionally. Stir in ⅓ cup water and next 5 ingredients; cover and simmer 4 minutes.

3. Place pasta evenly on each of 4 plates. Top pasta evenly with zucchini mixture and cheese. **Yield:** 4 servings (serving size: about ⅔ cup pasta, 1 cup zucchini mixture, and 2 tablespoons cheese).

Per serving: CALORIES 311; FAT 4.1g (sat 2.4g, mono 0.8g, poly 0.5g); PROTEIN 14.7g; CARB 55.3g; FIBER 7.5g; CHOL 13mg; IRON 3.3mg; SODIUM 452mg; CALC 147mg

Mixed Greens with Honey-Dijon Vinaigrette

prep: 7 minutes   *PointsPlus* value per serving: 2

    2   tablespoons balsamic vinegar
    1   tablespoon extra-virgin olive oil
    1   teaspoon honey
    ¼   teaspoon Dijon mustard
    ⅛   teaspoon coarsely ground black pepper
    4   cups torn mixed salad greens
    ½   cup seedless red grape halves

1. Combine first 5 ingredients in a large bowl, stirring with a whisk. Add greens; toss gently. Divide greens mixture among 4 plates; top evenly with grape halves. **Yield:** 4 servings (serving size: about 1 cup salad and 2 tablespoons grapes).

Per serving: CALORIES 66; FAT 3.7g (sat 0.5g, mono 2.5g, poly 0.6g); PROTEIN 1.1g; CARB 8.2g; FIBER 1.4g; CHOL 0mg; IRON 0.9mg; SODIUM 24mg; CALC 35mg

---

Menu
PointsPlus value
per serving: 10

Spaghetti with Zucchini and White Beans

Mixed Greens with Honey-Dijon Vinaigrette

Game Plan

1. While spaghetti cooks:
• Sauté zucchini.

2. While zucchini mixture cooks:
• Toss salad.

3. Combine pasta and vegetables.

Menu
PointsPlus value
per serving: 7

Meatless Meatballs over
Herbed Spaghetti Squash

1 cup mixed baby salad greens
with fat-free vinaigrette
PointsPlus value
per serving: 0

Game Plan

1. While squash cooks:
• Sauté onion, meatballs,
pesto, and sauce.

2. Remove strands from
squash, and season.

3. Combine meatballs, sauce,
and squash.

4. Toss salad.

Meatless Meatballs over Herbed Spaghetti Squash

prep: 7 minutes • **cook:** 14 minutes   *PointsPlus* value per serving: 7

Reminiscent of classic spaghetti and meatballs, this meatless recipe will please both vegetarians and meat lovers.

Cooking spray
1 (8-ounce) container prechopped onion
1 (12-ounce) package frozen zesty Italian-flavored meatless meatballs (such as Nate's)
1 (26-ounce) jar fire-roasted tomato-garlic pasta sauce (such as Classico)
2 tablespoons sun-dried tomato pesto (such as Classico)
Herbed Spaghetti Squash
Shredded fresh Parmesan cheese (optional)

1. Heat a large saucepan over medium-high heat; coat pan with cooking spray. Add onion; sauté 3 to 4 minutes or until tender. Add meatballs, pasta sauce, and pesto to pan; bring to a boil. Reduce heat; simmer 10 minutes or until meatballs are thoroughly heated. Spoon meatballs and sauce over Herbed Spaghetti Squash, and sprinkle with Parmesan cheese, if desired. **Yield:** 4 servings (serving size: about 1 cup meatball-sauce mixture and about 1 cup Herbed Spaghetti Squash).

Per serving: CALORIES 272; FAT 10.6g (sat 1g, mono 4.8g, poly 4g); PROTEIN 15.5g; CARB 30.8g; FIBER 5.3g; CHOL 0mg; IRON 4mg; SODIUM 1082mg; CALC 167mg

Herbed Spaghetti Squash

prep: 6 minutes • **cook:** 13 minutes   *PointsPlus* value per serving: 2

1 (3¼-pound) spaghetti squash
½ cup water
1 tablespoon extra-virgin olive oil
2 tablespoons chopped fresh basil
½ teaspoon salt
¼ teaspoon freshly ground black pepper

1. Pierce squash several times with the tip of a sharp knife. Microwave at HIGH 3 minutes. Cut squash in half lengthwise, and remove seeds and membrane with a spoon.
2. Place squash halves in an 11 x 7–inch baking dish (squash halves will overlap); add ½ cup water. Cover with plastic wrap; vent. Microwave at HIGH 10 minutes or until tender. Using a fork, remove spaghettilike strands, and place in a large bowl. Add olive oil and remaining ingredients; toss well. **Yield:** 4 servings (serving size: about 1 cup).

Per serving: CALORIES 76; FAT 3.3g (sat 0.5g, mono 1.9g, poly 1g); PROTEIN 0.6g; CARB 12.2g; FIBER 0.1g; CHOL 0mg; IRON 1mg; SODIUM 223mg; CALC 42mg

Zucchini-Potato Pancakes with Eggs

prep: 4 minutes • **cook:** 13 minutes   *PointsPlus* value per serving: 6

2   cups refrigerated shredded hash brown potatoes (such as Simply Potatoes)
1   cup shredded zucchini (about 1 small)
¼   cup Italian-seasoned panko (Japanese breadcrumbs)
¼   cup (1 ounce) shredded fresh Parmesan cheese
¼   teaspoon freshly ground black pepper
4   large egg whites, lightly beaten
Cooking spray
4   large eggs
⅛   teaspoon freshly ground black pepper

1. Combine first 6 ingredients in a large bowl.
2. Heat a large nonstick skillet over medium heat; heavily coat pan with cooking spray. Spoon about ½ cup potato mixture into 2 (5-inch) circles in pan. Cook 5 minutes; turn and cook 4 minutes or until potato is tender. Remove pancakes from pan, and keep warm. Repeat procedure with remaining potato mixture.
3. Reheat pan over medium-high heat; heavily recoat pan with cooking spray. Crack 4 eggs into pan; sprinkle with ⅛ teaspoon black pepper, and coat tops of eggs with cooking spray. Cover and cook 3 minutes or until whites have just set and yolks begin to thicken but are not hard or until desired degree of doneness. Slide 1 egg onto each pancake. **Yield:** 4 servings (serving size: 1 pancake and 1 egg).

Per serving: CALORIES 222; FAT 6.5g (sat 2.5g, mono 1.9g, poly 0.8g); PROTEIN 15.6g; CARB 24g; FIBER 1.6g; CHOL 186mg; IRON 1.4mg; SODIUM 392mg; CALC 120mg

Spinach Salad with Strawberries

prep: 4 minutes   *PointsPlus* value per serving: 3

1   tablespoon olive oil
1   tablespoon fresh lemon juice
1   teaspoon honey
¼   teaspoon salt
⅛   teaspoon black pepper
3   cups bagged baby spinach leaves
1   cup quartered strawberries
⅓   cup (1.3 ounces) crumbled feta cheese (optional)

1. Combine first 5 ingredients in a large bowl, stirring well with a whisk. Add spinach and strawberries; toss well. Sprinkle with feta cheese, if desired. **Yield:** 2 servings (serving size: 2 cups).

Per serving: CALORIES 108; FAT 7g (sat 0.9g, mono 5g, poly 0.8g); PROTEIN 1.5g; CARB 11.3g; FIBER 2.6g; CHOL 0mg; IRON 2mg; SODIUM 320mg; CALC 49mg

---

Menu
PointsPlus value
per serving: 9

Zucchini-Potato Pancake with Egg

Spinach Salad with Strawberries

Game Plan

1. Combine ingredients for zucchini pancakes.

2. While pancakes cook:
• Prepare salad dressing.

3. Cook eggs, and top pancakes.

4. Assemble salad.

Menu
PointsPlus value
per serving: 11

Spinach and Roasted Red Bell
Pepper Tart

1/2 cup microwave roasted
potatoes (such as Birds Eye)
PointsPlus value
per serving: 2

Game Plan

1. While oven preheats:
- Prepare pie dough.
- Drain spinach.

2. While crust bakes:
- Combine vegetables and
cheese.
- Combine eggs.

3. Assemble tart.

4. While tart bakes:
- Prepare potatoes
according to package
directions.

Spinach and Roasted Red Bell Pepper Tart

prep: 4 minutes • **cook:** 51 minutes   *PointsPlus* value per serving: 9

Pan-roasted potatoes make a hearty side dish for this savory tart. Take care not to stretch the dough while you are fitting it into the tart pan as this will cause it to shrink and fall away from the sides of the pan as it bakes.

 1/2 (15-ounce) package refrigerated pie dough (such as Pillsbury)
      Cooking spray
 1   (10-ounce) package frozen leaf spinach and butter sauce (such as Green
      Giant), thawed and drained
 1/2 cup chopped bottled roasted red bell peppers
 1/2 cup (2 ounces) reduced-fat crumbled feta cheese with basil and sun-dried
      tomatoes
 3/4 cup egg substitute
 1/4 teaspoon salt
 1/4 teaspoon freshly ground black pepper

1. Preheat oven to 400°.

2. Unroll dough, and roll into a 12-inch circle. Fit dough into a 9-inch round removable-bottom tart pan coated with cooking spray; press dough against sides of pan. Pierce bottom and sides of dough with a fork. Place pan on bottom rack in oven. Bake at 400° for 14 minutes or until golden.

3. While crust bakes, combine spinach, bell peppers, and cheese in a bowl. Combine egg substitute, salt, and black pepper in another bowl.

4. Remove crust from oven; sprinkle spinach mixture over bottom of crust. Pour egg substitute mixture over spinach mixture. Return tart to bottom rack. Bake an additional 37 minutes or until crust is golden brown and custard is set. Cut into 8 wedges. **Yield:** 4 servings (serving size: 2 wedges).

Per serving: CALORIES 342; FAT 18.9g (sat 7.9g, mono 5g, poly 5g); PROTEIN 10g; CARB 31.8g; FIBER 1.5g; CHOL 21mg; IRON 2mg; SODIUM 908mg; CALC 138mg

pictured on page 41

Mushroom Stroganoff

prep: 2 minutes • **cook:** 13 minutes   *PointsPlus* value per serving: 10

We used a blend of oyster, shiitake, and baby bella mushrooms in this superb vegetarian stroganoff. Browning the mushrooms over high heat ensures that they develop rich flavor.

3½ cups uncooked medium egg noodles
   Butter-flavored cooking spray
  5 (4-ounce) packages fresh gourmet-blend mushrooms
  1 cup coarsely chopped onion
  3 tablespoons all-purpose flour
1½ cups 2% reduced-fat milk
  3 tablespoons dry sherry
  2 tablespoons light butter, melted
  ½ teaspoon salt
  ½ teaspoon freshly ground black pepper
  ½ cup reduced-fat sour cream
1½ tablespoons finely chopped chives (optional)

1. Cook noodles according to package directions, omitting salt and fat; drain.
2. While noodles cook, heat a large Dutch oven over high heat; generously coat pan with cooking spray. Add mushrooms and onion; cook 10 minutes or until browned, stirring frequently.
3. While mushroom mixture cooks, place flour in a bowl. Gradually add milk, stirring with a whisk until smooth. Add sherry and next 3 ingredients, stirring with a whisk. Transfer cooked mushroom mixture to a large bowl. Gradually add milk mixture to hot pan, stirring with a whisk. Cook, whisking constantly, 3 minutes or until slightly thick.
4. Stir sauce and cooked noodles into mushroom mixture. Stir in sour cream; sprinkle with chives, if desired. Serve immediately. **Yield:** 4 servings (serving size: 1¾ cups).

Per serving: CALORIES 393; FAT 12.6g (sat 6.5g, mono 3.6g, poly 2g); PROTEIN 15g; CARB 55.2g; FIBER 3.5g; CHOL 83mg; IRON 3.8mg; SODIUM 400mg; CALC 162mg

---

Menu
PointsPlus value
per serving: 10

Mushroom Stroganoff

1 cup steamed broccoli
PointsPlus value
per serving: 0

Game Plan

1. While noodles cook:
  • Cook mushrooms and onions.
  • Combine milk, sherry, butter, and spices.
  • Steam broccoli.

2. Heat and thicken milk mixture.

3. Combine stroganoff.

Menu
PointsPlus value
per serving: 7

**Grilled Stuffed Portobello
Mushroom**

Grilled Tomato Salad

Game Plan

1. While grill heats:
• Prepare mushrooms and
spinach mixture.

2. Grill mushrooms and
tomatoes.

3. Assemble salad.

Grilled Stuffed Portobello Mushrooms

prep: 5 minutes • **cook:** 10 minutes   *PointsPlus* value per serving: 6

 2 (4½-inch) portobello mushroom caps
 2 teaspoons olive oil, divided
 1 garlic clove, minced
 ¾ cup minced onion (1 small)
 1½ teaspoons chopped fresh oregano
 ½ cup bagged baby spinach leaves
 ¼ cup grated Parmesan cheese
 ⅓ cup Italian-seasoned panko (Japanese breadcrumbs)
 1½ teaspoons balsamic vinegar
 ½ teaspoon black pepper

1. Prepare grill.
2. Remove brown gills from undersides of mushrooms using a spoon; discard gills. Set mushroom caps aside.
3. Heat 1 teaspoon oil in a large nonstick skillet over medium-high heat. Add mushroom caps, garlic, and onion; sauté 2 minutes. Add oregano and spinach; sauté 1 minute or until spinach wilts.
4. Transfer spinach mixture to a medium bowl; stir in remaining 1 teaspoon oil, cheese, panko, vinegar, and pepper. Divide filling evenly among mushrooms, spooning onto gill sides.
5. Grill 7 minutes. **Yield:** 2 servings (serving size: 1 mushroom cap).

Per serving: CALORIES 216; FAT 8.6g (sat 2.7g, mono 4.1g, poly 1g); PROTEIN 9.6g; CARB 25.3g; FIBER 3.2g; CHOL 9mg; IRON 1mg; SODIUM 300mg; CALC 146mg

Grilled Tomato Salad

prep: 3 minutes • **cook:** 6 minutes   *PointsPlus* value per serving: 1

 2 plum tomatoes, quartered
 Cooking spray
 ¼ cup small fresh basil leaves
 1 teaspoon olive oil
 1 teaspoon balsamic vinegar
 ⅛ teaspoon salt

1. Prepare grill.
2. Place tomatoes on grill rack coated with cooking spray. Grill 3 minutes on each side. Place tomatoes in a bowl; add basil and remaining ingredients, tossing to coat. **Yield:** 2 servings (serving size: 4 tomato quarters).

Per serving: CALORIES 36; FAT 2.4g (sat 0.4g, mono 1.6g, poly 0.4g); PROTEIN 0.6g; CARB 3.6g; FIBER 0.8g; CHOL 0mg; IRON 0.4mg; SODIUM 152mg; CALC 12mg

Meats

Menu
PointsPlus value
per serving: 9

Mozzarella-Stuffed Meat Loaf

½ cup precooked rice
PointsPlus value
per serving: 3

1 cup steamed green beans
PointsPlus value
per serving: 0

Game Plan

1. While oven preheats:
• Prepare individual meat
  loaves.

2. While meat loaves cook:
• Steam green beans.
• Heat rice.

Mozzarella-Stuffed Meat Loaves

prep: 9 minutes • **cook:** 45 minutes   *PointsPlus* value per serving: 6

Soft, melted mozzarella oozes out when you cut into this classic comfort food. Serve with mashed potatoes and steamed green beans for the ultimate comfort meal.

Cooking spray
1 large egg
¾ cup tomato-basil pasta sauce (such as Classico), divided
¼ teaspoon salt
¼ teaspoon black pepper
1 pound ground sirloin
⅓ cup uncooked quick-cooking oats
¾ cup (3 ounces) shredded part-skim mozzarella cheese

1. Preheat oven to 350°.
2. Line bottom of a broiler pan with foil; coat rack with cooking spray. Place egg in a large bowl, stirring well with a whisk. Add ¼ cup pasta sauce, salt, and pepper, stirring with a whisk until blended. Add beef and oats. Using hands, gently mix just until blended. Divide meat mixture into 4 equal portions; place 3 tablespoons cheese in middle of each portion. Shape meat around cheese to form a small loaf. Place loaves on rack of prepared pan. Spread 1 tablespoon pasta sauce over each loaf.
3. Bake at 350° for 35 minutes; spoon remaining ¼ cup pasta sauce over meat loaves. Bake an additional 10 minutes or until a thermometer registers 160°.
Yield: 4 servings (serving size: 1 loaf).

Per serving: CALORIES 257; FAT 11.1g (sat 3.5g, mono 4g, poly 1.8g); PROTEIN 30.6g; CARB 8.3g; FIBER 1.5g; CHOL 113mg; IRON 2.8mg; SODIUM 464mg; CALC 42mg

Smothered Pepper Steak

prep: 4 minutes • **cook:** 25 minutes   *PointsPlus* value per serving: 6

To capture all of its saucy flavor, plate this quick weeknight family favorite over hot cooked rice.

- 3 tablespoons all-purpose flour
- 4 (4-ounce) ground sirloin patties
- ¼ teaspoon salt
- ¼ teaspoon black pepper
- Cooking spray
- 1 (16-ounce) package frozen bell pepper stir-fry (such as Birds Eye)
- 1 (14.5-ounce) can diced tomatoes with balsamic vinegar, basil, and olive oil (such as Hunt's), undrained
- 1 tablespoon lower-sodium soy sauce

1. Place flour in a shallow dish. Dredge sirloin patties in flour; sprinkle patties evenly with salt and black pepper. Heat a large nonstick skillet over medium-high heat. Coat pan with cooking spray. Coat patties with cooking spray. Add patties to pan; cook 3 minutes on each side or until lightly browned.
2. Add stir-fry, tomatoes, and soy sauce to meat in pan; bring to a boil. Reduce heat; simmer 15 minutes or until meat is done and bell pepper mixture is slightly thick. **Yield:** 4 servings (serving size: 1 sirloin patty and about ¾ cup sauce).

Per serving: CALORIES 246; FAT 8g (sat 2g, mono 2g, poly 0.5g); PROTEIN 25.1g; CARB 18.2g; FIBER 2g; CHOL 60mg; IRON 2.7mg; SODIUM 785mg; CALC 52mg

Menu
PointsPlus value
per serving: 14

Smothered Pepper Steak

½ cup precooked brown rice
PointsPlus value
per serving: 3

Chocolate-Peppermint
Parfaits

Game Plan

1. Dredge and season sirloin patties.

2. Brown patties, and add remaining ingredients.

3. While pepper steak simmers:
• Heat rice.

4. Prepare parfaits.

Chocolate-Peppermint Parfaits

prep: 8 minutes   *PointsPlus* value per serving: 5

- 1 cup coarsely chopped vanilla meringue cookies (such as Miss Meringue; about 4 cookies)
- 2 cups chocolate low-fat ice cream (such as Edy's)
- 1 cup refrigerated canned light whipped topping (such as Reddi-wip)
- ½ cup finely crushed soft peppermint candies

1. Spoon ¼ cup cookies into each of 4 parfait glasses; top each serving with ¼ cup ice cream, 2 tablespoons whipped topping, and 1 tablespoon peppermint candies. Repeat layers with remaining ice cream, whipped topping, and peppermint candies. **Yield:** 4 servings (serving size: 1 parfait).

Per serving: CALORIES 222; FAT 4g (sat 2g, mono 0g, poly 0g); PROTEIN 2.1g; CARB 39.3g; FIBER 0g; CHOL 11mg; IRON 0.4mg; SODIUM 57mg; CALC 80mg

Menu

PointsPlus value
per serving: 9

Mongolian Beef

¹/₂ cup boil-in-bag jasmine rice
PointsPlus value
per serving: 3

1 cup steamed snow peas
PointsPlus value
per serving: 0

Game Plan

1. While skillet heats:
• Peel and mince ginger;
cut onions.
• Boil water for rice.

2. While steak cooks:
• Steam snow peas.
• Combine sauce.
• Prepare rice.

3. Prepare sauce.

Mongolian Beef

prep: 4 minutes • **cook:** 6 minutes   *PointsPlus* value per serving: 6

This spicy Asian favorite gets its flavor from hoisin sauce and dark sesame oil. Hoisin sauce is a versatile, sweet-and-spicy condiment that is used in Chinese cooking and dining much the same way Westerners use ketchup. The dark sesame oil imparts a distinctive nutty taste and aroma to the dish. Serve with boil-in-bag jasmine rice and steamed snow peas.

    1   (1-pound) flank steak, trimmed and cut into thin slices
        Butter-flavored cooking spray
    ¹/₃ cup hoisin sauce
    2   tablespoons water
    2   teaspoons minced peeled fresh ginger
    1   teaspoon bottled minced roasted garlic
    2   teaspoons dark sesame oil
    ¹/₂ teaspoon crushed red pepper
    4   green onions

1. Heat a large nonstick skillet over medium-high heat. Coat steak with cooking spray. Cook steak in pan over medium-high heat 3 minutes or until browned and liquid has almost evaporated, stirring occasionally.

2. While steak cooks, combine hoisin sauce and next 5 ingredients in a small bowl. Cut onions crosswise into 1-inch pieces. Add sauce mixture and onions to meat in pan; cook 1 to 2 minutes or until sauce is slightly reduced (do not overcook meat). Serve immediately. Yield: 4 servings (serving size: about ½ cup).

Per serving: CALORIES 240; FAT 10g (sat 2.8g, mono 3.4g, poly 2.6g); PROTEIN 25.5g; CARB 11.1g; FIBER 1.1g; CHOL 38mg; IRON 2.2mg; SODIUM 410mg; CALC 45mg

pictured on page 42

Orange Beef and Broccoli

prep: 7 minutes • **cook:** 7 minutes   *PointsPlus* value per serving: 6

For convenience, ask the butcher to cut the steak into thin slices.

- 1 (12-ounce) package refrigerated broccoli florets
- ⅓ cup fat-free, lower-sodium beef broth
- ⅓ cup low-sugar orange marmalade
- 2 tablespoons lower-sodium soy sauce
- ¼ teaspoon salt
- 2 tablespoons cornstarch
- 1 (1-pound) flank steak, trimmed and cut into thin slices
- Cooking spray

1. Microwave broccoli according to package directions.
2. While broccoli cooks, combine broth and next 3 ingredients in a small bowl, stirring with a whisk; set aside.
3. Place cornstarch in a shallow dish. Dredge steak in cornstarch.
4. Heat a large nonstick skillet over medium-high heat. Coat pan with cooking spray. Add steak; sauté 5 minutes or until browned on all sides. Add broth mixture; cook 1 minute or until thick. Stir in broccoli. Serve immediately. **Yield:** 4 servings (serving size: 1 cup).

Per serving: CALORIES 238; FAT 7g (sat 2.4g, mono 2.2g, poly 0.4g); PROTEIN 27.7g; CARB 16.6g; FIBER 2.5g; CHOL 37mg; IRON 2.6mg; SODIUM 570mg; CALC 68mg

Wasabi Ice Cream with Honey

prep: 4 minutes • **cook:** 4 minutes • **other:** 2 hours and 46 minutes
PointsPlus value per serving: 5

- 1½ cups water
- ¾ cup sugar
- 1 tablespoon wasabi paste
- 4 teaspoons lemon juice
- 1¼ cups whole milk
- 3 tablespoons honey

1. Combine 1½ cups water and sugar in a saucepan; bring to a boil, stirring until sugar dissolves. Remove pan from heat; add wasabi paste and lemon juice, stirring with a whisk. Cover and chill completely.
2. Stir in milk. Pour mixture into the freezer can of an ice cream freezer; freeze according to manufacturer's instructions. Spoon ice cream into a freezer-safe container; cover and freeze 1 hour or until firm. Drizzle each serving with honey. **Yield:** 6 servings (serving size: about ½ cup ice cream and 1½ teaspoons honey).

Per serving: CALORIES 178; FAT 2g (sat 1g, mono 0.4g, poly 0.1g); PROTEIN 1.7g; CARB 37.7g; FIBER 0g; CHOL 5mg; IRON 0.1mg; SODIUM 71mg; CALC 59mg

---

Menu
PointsPlus value
per serving: 14

Orange Beef and Broccoli

½ cup precooked rice
PointsPlus value
per serving: 3

Wasabi Ice Cream with Honey

Game Plan

1. Prepare ice cream, and freeze.

2. While broccoli cooks:
• Combine orange sauce.

3. While skillet heats:
• Dredge meat.

4. Sauté steak with sauce and broccoli.

5. Heat rice.

pictured on page 43

Mustard-Molasses Flank Steak

prep: 4 minutes • **cook:** 10 minutes • **other:** 30 minutes
PointsPlus value per serving: 5

⅓ cup balsamic vinegar
¼ cup fat-free, lower-sodium beef broth
2 tablespoons molasses
2 tablespoons whole-grain Dijon mustard
¼ teaspoon salt
¼ teaspoon freshly ground black pepper
1 (1-pound) flank steak, trimmed
Cooking spray

1. Combine first 7 ingredients in a large zip-top plastic bag; seal. Marinate in refrigerator 30 minutes. Preheat broiler.
2. Remove steak from bag, reserving marinade. Place steak on a broiler pan coated with cooking spray; broil 5 minutes on each side or until desired degree of doneness. Remove steak from oven; cover loosely with foil.
3. While steak broils, place reserved marinade in a small nonstick skillet. Bring to a boil; cook until reduced to ⅓ cup (about 6 minutes), stirring occasionally.
4. Cut steak diagonally across the grain into ¼-inch-thick slices. Drizzle mustard-molasses sauce over steak. **Yield:** 4 servings (serving size: 3 ounces steak and about 1½ tablespoons sauce).

Per serving: CALORIES 219; FAT 7g (sat 2.3g, mono 2.2g, poly 0.2g); PROTEIN 25.2g; CARB 12.4g; FIBER 0.3g; CHOL 37mg; IRON 2.6mg; SODIUM 397mg; CALC 60mg

Sweet Potatoes with Orange-Thyme Butter

prep: 3 minutes • **cook:** 8 minutes   *PointsPlus* value per serving: 4

4 (6-ounce) sweet potatoes
2 tablespoons butter, softened
2 teaspoons grated orange rind
1 teaspoon chopped fresh thyme
¼ teaspoon freshly ground black pepper
⅛ teaspoon salt

1. Scrub potatoes; place in a bowl (do not pierce potatoes). Cover bowl with plastic wrap (do not allow plastic wrap to touch food); vent. Microwave at HIGH 8 minutes or until done. While potatoes cook, combine butter and next 4 ingredients in a bowl.
2. Cut each potato lengthwise; fluff with a fork. Top each potato evenly with butter mixture. **Yield:** 4 servings (serving size: 1 sweet potato and 2¼ teaspoons butter).

Per serving: CALORIES 145; FAT 6g (sat 3.6g, mono 1.5g, poly 0.3g); PROTEIN 2.2g; CARB 21.8g; FIBER 3.6g; CHOL 15mg; IRON 0.8mg; SODIUM 150mg; CALC 44mg

---

Menu
PointsPlus value
per serving: 9

Mustard-Molasses Flank Steak

Sweet Potatoes with Orange-Thyme Butter

Game Plan

1. Prepare marinade.

2. While steak marinates:
• Preheat broiler.
• Scrub sweet potatoes.

3. While steak grills:
• Microwave sweet potatoes.
• Reduce marinade.
• Combine butter mixture.

Beef Tenderloin Steaks with Red Wine–Mushroom Sauce

prep: 1 minute • **cook:** 10 minutes　　　　*PointsPlus* value per serving: 8

```
4   (4-ounce) beef tenderloin steaks, trimmed (about ½ inch thick)
¼   teaspoon salt
¼   teaspoon freshly ground black pepper
    Butter-flavored cooking spray
1   (8-ounce) package presliced baby portobello mushrooms
1   cup dry red wine
2   tablespoons butter
1   teaspoon minced fresh rosemary
```

1. Heat a large nonstick skillet over medium-high heat. Sprinkle steaks with salt and pepper; coat with cooking spray. Add steaks to pan; cook 3 minutes on each side or until desired degree of doneness. Transfer steaks to a serving platter; keep warm.
2. Add mushrooms to pan. Coat mushrooms with cooking spray; sauté 3 minutes or until browned. Stir in wine, scraping pan to loosen browned bits. Cook until liquid almost evaporates. Remove pan from heat; add butter and rosemary, stirring until butter melts. Pour sauce over steaks. **Yield:** 4 servings (serving size: 1 steak and ¼ cup sauce).

Per serving: CALORIES 244; FAT 13g (sat 6g, mono 4g, poly 0.9g); PROTEIN 23.3g; CARB 3.8g; FIBER 0.9g; CHOL 74mg; IRON 1.9mg; SODIUM 235mg; CALC 24mg

Menu
PointsPlus value per serving: 10

Beef Tenderloin Steak with Red Wine–Mushroom Sauce

Wedge Salad with Sour Cream–Mustard Seed Dressing

Game Plan

1. While steaks cook:
  • Prepare salad dressing.
  • Rinse and dice tomatoes.

2. While mushrooms and wine cook:
  • Assemble salad.

3. Add butter to sauce, and top steaks.

Wedge Salad with Sour Cream–Mustard Seed Dressing

prep: 6 minutes　　　　*PointsPlus* value per serving: 2

```
⅓   cup reduced-fat sour cream
3   tablespoons water
2   tablespoons light mayonnaise
2   teaspoons whole-grain Dijon mustard
⅛   teaspoon salt
1   garlic clove, minced
½   head iceberg lettuce, cut into 4 wedges
½   cup diced plum tomato (about 1 tomato)
    Freshly ground black pepper
```

1. Combine first 6 ingredients in a medium bowl, stirring well with a whisk.
2. Place 1 lettuce wedge on each of 4 plates. Drizzle with dressing. Top with tomato and pepper. **Yield:** 4 servings (serving size: 1 lettuce wedge, about 3 tablespoons dressing, and 2 tablespoons tomato).

Per serving: CALORIES 73; FAT 5g (sat 2g, mono 0.7g, poly 2.4g); PROTEIN 1.8g; CARB 5.5g; FIBER 1g; CHOL 13mg; IRON 0.4mg; SODIUM 212mg; CALC 49mg

pictured on page 44

Slow-Cooker Beef Pot Roast

prep: 4 minutes • **cook:** 7 hours and 7 minutes   *PointsPlus* value per serving: 6

Pair this home-style favorite with mashed potatoes to soak up the sauce. Leftover pot roast makes great hot roast beef sandwiches the next day.

  1 (8-ounce) package presliced mushrooms
  1 (8-ounce) container refrigerated prechopped green bell pepper
Cooking spray
¼ cup plus 2 tablespoons ketchup
¼ cup water
  1 tablespoon Worcestershire sauce
½ teaspoon black pepper
¼ teaspoon salt
  2 pounds boneless shoulder pot roast

1. Place mushrooms and bell pepper in a 3½- to 4-quart electric slow cooker coated with cooking spray.
2. Combine ketchup and next 4 ingredients in a small bowl, stirring until blended.
3. Heat a large nonstick skillet over medium-high heat. Coat pan and roast with cooking spray. Cook 3 minutes on each side or until browned. Place roast over vegetables in cooker; pour ketchup mixture over roast. Cover and cook on HIGH for 1 hour. Reduce heat to LOW; cook 6 to 7 hours or until roast is very tender. Serve vegetables and sauce over roast. Yield: 6 servings (serving size: 3 ounces beef and ½ cup vegetables and sauce).

Per serving: CALORIES 228; FAT 8g (sat 2g, mono 3.1g, poly 0.1g); PROTEIN 31.3g; CARB 7.4g; FIBER 1.1g; CHOL 89mg; IRON 4.2mg; SODIUM 397mg; CALC 21mg

Menu
PointsPlus value
per serving: 9

Slow-Cooker Beef Pot Roast

½ cup microwave
mashed potatoes
PointsPlus value
per serving: 3

Game Plan

1. Blend sauce.

2. Brown roast, and add to slow cooker with vegetables.

3. Slow-cook roast.

4. Five minutes before serving roast:
  • Prepare mashed potatoes according to package directions.

Spiced Pork Chops with Butternut Squash

prep: 4 minutes • cook: 21 minutes   *PointsPlus* value per serving: 6

Cooking spray
4   (4-ounce) boneless center-cut loin pork chops (about ¾ inch thick)
1   teaspoon pumpkin pie spice
½   teaspoon freshly ground black pepper
¼   teaspoon salt, divided
1   butternut squash (about 1¼ pounds)
1   cup refrigerated prechopped onion
¼   cup water
1   tablespoon chopped fresh mint

1. Heat a large nonstick skillet over medium-high heat. Coat pan with cooking spray. Sprinkle pork evenly with spice, pepper, and ⅛ teaspoon salt. Add pork to pan; sauté 3 to 4 minutes on each side or until done. Remove pork from pan; keep warm.
2. While pork cooks, pierce squash several times with a fork; place on paper towels in microwave oven. Microwave at HIGH 1 minute. Peel squash; cut in half lengthwise. Discard seeds and membrane. Coarsely chop squash.
3. Coat pan with cooking spray. Add squash; cover and cook 7 minutes, stirring occasionally. Add onion; cook, uncovered, 5 minutes, stirring frequently. Add ¼ cup water; cook until liquid evaporates, scraping pan to loosen browned bits. Remove from heat; stir in remaining ⅛ teaspoon salt and mint. Spoon squash mixture evenly over pork. **Yield:** 4 servings (serving size: 1 pork chop and ¾ cup squash).

Per serving: CALORIES 232; FAT 7g (sat 2.4g, mono 2.9g, poly 0.5g); PROTEIN 25.6g; CARB 18.2g; FIBER 3.2g; CHOL 65mg; IRON 1.7mg; SODIUM 200mg; CALC 96mg

Ginger Couscous with Jalapeños and Cilantro

prep: 2 minutes • cook: 2 minutes • other: 5 minutes
PointsPlus value per serving: 2

⅔   cup uncooked whole-wheat couscous
1   jalapeño pepper, seeded and minced
2   tablespoons chopped fresh cilantro
1½ teaspoons grated peeled fresh ginger
2   teaspoons canola oil
¼   teaspoon salt

1. Prepare couscous according to package directions for 2 servings, omitting salt and fat. Fluff with a fork; stir in jalapeño pepper and remaining ingredients. **Yield:** 4 servings (serving size: about ½ cup).

Per serving: CALORIES 92; FAT 3g (sat 0.2g, mono 1.4g, poly 0.7g); PROTEIN 2.7g; CARB 15.4g; FIBER 2.5g; CHOL 0mg; IRON 0.6mg; SODIUM 146mg; CALC 8mg

---

Menu
PointsPlus value
per serving: 8

**Spiced Pork Chop with
Butternut Squash**

**Ginger Couscous with
Jalapeños and Cilantro**

Game Plan

1. While pork cooks:
• Microwave, peel, and chop squash.

2. While squash and onion sauté:
• Prepare couscous.
• Seed and mince jalapeños.
• Chop cilantro.
• Grate ginger.

3. Combine squash and pork.

4. Mix jalapeños, ginger, cilantro, and couscous.

pictured on page 45

Menu
PointsPlus value
per serving: 6

Lemon-Herb Skillet
Pork Chop

Sweet Pea and Bell
Pepper Toss

Game Plan

1. While oil heats:
• Season and dredge pork.

2. While pork cooks:
• Prepare Sweet Pea and
Bell Pepper Toss.

Lemon-Herb Skillet Pork Chops

prep: 2 minutes • **cook:** 11 minutes   *PointsPlus* value per serving: 5

A squeeze of fresh lemon completes the dish and provides a hint of tartness that enhances the natural mild sweetness of the chops.

- 4 (4-ounce) boneless center-cut loin pork chops (about ½ inch thick)
- ½ teaspoon salt
- ½ teaspoon black pepper
- 3 tablespoons all-purpose flour
- ¾ teaspoon dried thyme
- ¾ teaspoon paprika
- ¼ teaspoon dried rubbed sage
- 1 tablespoon olive oil
- 4 lemon wedges

1. Sprinkle both sides of pork evenly with salt and pepper. Combine flour and next 3 ingredients in a shallow dish. Dredge pork in flour mixture.
2. Heat oil in a large nonstick skillet over medium-high heat. Add pork; cook 4 minutes on each side or until pork is done. Serve with lemon wedges. **Yield:** 4 servings (serving size: 1 pork chop and 1 lemon wedge).

Per serving: CALORIES 218; FAT 10g (sat 2.9g, mono 5.4g, poly 1g); PROTEIN 24.7g; CARB 5.9g; FIBER 0.7g; CHOL 65mg; IRON 1.1mg; SODIUM 340mg; CALC 41mg

Sweet Pea and Bell Pepper Toss

prep: 1 minute • **cook:** 7 minutes   *PointsPlus* value per serving: 1

  Cooking spray
- 1 cup refrigerated prechopped onion
- 1 cup refrigerated prechopped tricolor bell pepper
- 1 cup frozen petite green peas
- ¼ teaspoon salt

1. Heat a large nonstick skillet over medium-high heat. Coat pan with cooking spray. Add onion to pan; coat with cooking spray. Cook 2 minutes. Add bell pepper; coat with cooking spray. Cook 3 minutes or until vegetables are tender and lightly browned, stirring frequently.
2. Stir in peas and salt; cook 1 to 2 minutes or until thoroughly heated, stirring frequently. **Yield:** 4 servings (serving size: ½ cup).

Per serving: CALORIES 34; FAT 0g (sat 0g, mono 0g, poly 0.1g); PROTEIN 1.4g; CARB 7.5g; FIBER 1.7g; CHOL 0mg; IRON 0.4mg; SODIUM 160mg; CALC 15mg

Curried Pork and Chai Rice

prep: 3 minutes • **cook:** 12 minutes • **other:** 5 minutes
PointsPlus value per serving: 6

Delight your palate by cooking with chai tea. Chai is a fragrantly spiced, sweetened black tea served in India. It typically includes a combination of cinnamon, cloves, cardamom, and black peppercorns.

  1 large navel orange
  ¾ cup plus 2 tablespoons water
  2 spiced chai tea bags
  1 cup uncooked instant brown rice
  ½ teaspoon salt, divided
  4 (4-ounce) boneless center-cut loin pork chops (about ½ inch thick)
  1 teaspoon curry powder
  ¼ teaspoon ground cumin (optional)
     Cooking spray

1. Grate rind from orange to measure 1 teaspoon. Squeeze juice from orange to measure 6 tablespoons. Combine 2 tablespoons orange juice, ¾ cup plus 2 tablespoons water, and tea bags in a medium saucepan; bring to a boil. Add rice; cover, reduce heat, and simmer 5 minutes. Remove from heat; let stand, covered, 5 minutes. Remove tea bags; stir in orange rind and ¼ teaspoon salt.

2. While rice cooks, sprinkle pork evenly with remaining ¼ teaspoon salt, curry powder, and, if desired, cumin. Heat a large nonstick skillet over medium-high heat. Coat pan with cooking spray. Add pork; cook 4 minutes on each side or until done. Transfer to a serving platter, and keep warm. Add remaining 4 tablespoons orange juice to pan; cook 1 minute, scraping pan to loosen browned bits or until reduced to 2 tablespoons. Drizzle sauce over pork; serve with rice. **Yield:** 4 servings (serving size: 1 pork chop and ½ cup rice).

Per serving: CALORIES 254; FAT 7g (sat 2.4g, mono 2.9g, poly 0.5g); PROTEIN 25.8g; CARB 22.2g; FIBER 2g; CHOL 65mg; IRON 1.1mg; SODIUM 344mg; CALC 43mg

Menu
PointsPlus value per serving: 6

Curried Pork and Chai Rice

1 cup steamed snow peas
PointsPlus value per serving: 0

Game Plan

1. Boil water, orange juice, and tea for rice.

2. While rice cooks:
  • Season and cook pork.
  • Steam snow peas.

3. Reduce orange juice sauce.

pictured on page 46

Sherried Pineapple Pork Tenderloin

prep: 1 minute • **cook:** 29 minutes • **other:** 3 minutes
PointsPlus value per serving: 5

Menu
PointsPlus value
per serving: 8

Sherried Pineapple Pork Tenderloin

Red Cabbage and Carrot Slaw

Game Plan

1. Season and brown pork.

2. While pork cooks:
 • Peel and grate ginger.
 • Combine and toss slaw.

3. While pork stands:
 • Combine and reduce sauce.

Impress your guests with this company-worthy main dish served alongside a colorful slaw.

½ teaspoon black pepper
1 (1-pound) pork tenderloin, trimmed
Cooking spray
1 (6-ounce) can pineapple juice
2 tablespoons sugar
2 tablespoons dry sherry
1 tablespoon lower-sodium soy sauce

1. Sprinkle pepper evenly over pork.
2. Heat a nonstick skillet over medium-high heat. Coat pan with cooking spray; add pork. Cook pork 3 to 4 minutes or until browned, turning occasionally. Reduce heat to medium-low; cover and cook 10 minutes. Turn pork over; cook 10 minutes or until a thermometer registers 160° (slightly pink).
3. Place pork on a cutting board; let stand 3 minutes. Cut into ¼-inch-thick slices.
4. While pork stands, combine pineapple juice and next 3 ingredients; add to pan drippings. Bring to a boil; boil 5 minutes or until liquid is reduced to ¼ cup. Spoon sauce over pork slices. **Yield:** 4 servings (serving size: 3 ounces pork and 1 tablespoon sauce).

Per serving: CALORIES 190; FAT 4g (sat 1.3g, mono 1.5g, poly 0.3g); PROTEIN 22.8g; CARB 13.5g; FIBER 0.1g; CHOL 63mg; IRON 1.3mg; SODIUM 243mg; CALC 6mg

Red Cabbage and Carrot Slaw

prep: 6 minutes   *PointsPlus* value per serving: 3

2 cups matchstick-cut carrots
¾ cup very thinly sliced red cabbage
½ cup refrigerated prechopped tricolor bell pepper
3 tablespoons unsalted, dry-roasted peanuts
2 tablespoons cider vinegar
1 teaspoon grated peeled fresh ginger
⅛ teaspoon salt

1. Combine all ingredients in a medium bowl, tossing gently to coat. **Yield:** 4 servings (serving size: ¾ cup).

Per serving: CALORIES 100; FAT 3g (sat 0.5g, mono 1.7g, poly 1.1g); PROTEIN 2.4g; CARB 16.1g; FIBER 1.9g; CHOL 0mg; IRON 0.5mg; SODIUM 78mg; CALC 20mg

Spinach, Pesto, and Feta–Stuffed Pork Tenderloin with Chunky Tomato Sauce

prep: 9 minutes • **cook:** 22 minutes • **other:** 5 minutes
PointsPlus value per serving: 6

Canned tomatoes spiked with balsamic vinegar and basil roast with the pork to create an easy sauce. Serve hot cooked orzo to soak up the juices.

  1 (1-pound) pork tenderloin, trimmed
  ¼ cup sun-dried tomato pesto (such as Classico)
  1 cup baby spinach
  ¼ cup (1 ounce) crumbled feta cheese with basil and sun-dried tomatoes
  Olive oil–flavored cooking spray
  ¼ teaspoon black pepper
  1 (14.5-ounce) can diced tomatoes with balsamic vinegar, basil, and olive oil (such as Hunt's), undrained

1. Preheat oven to 500°.

2. Cut pork lengthwise, cutting to, but not through, other side. Open halves, laying pork flat. Place pork halves between 2 sheets of heavy-duty plastic wrap; pound to an even thickness using a meat mallet or small heavy skillet. Spread pesto evenly down length of tenderloin; top with spinach and feta. Close tenderloin; secure at intervals with wooden picks (about 12). Place pork in a 13 x 9–inch baking pan coated with cooking spray. Coat pork with cooking spray; sprinkle evenly with pepper. Pour tomatoes around pork in pan.

3. Bake at 500° for 22 minutes or until a thermometer registers 160° (slightly pink). Let stand 5 minutes. Discard wooden picks; cut pork into 8 slices. Serve roasted tomatoes over pork. **Yield:** 4 servings (serving size: 3 ounces pork and about ⅓ cup tomato sauce).

Per serving: CALORIES 240; FAT 10g (sat 2.7g, mono 2.7g, poly 1.2g); PROTEIN 25.7g; CARB 9.7g; FIBER 1g; CHOL 69mg; IRON 2.3mg; SODIUM 702mg; CALC 83mg

Menu
PointsPlus value
per serving: 9

Spinach, Pesto, and Feta–
Stuffed Pork Tenderloin with
Chunky Tomato Sauce

½ cup cooked orzo pasta
PointsPlus value
per serving: 3

Game Plan

1. While oven preheats:
• Cut and pound pork.
• Top pork with pesto, feta, and spinach.
• Close pork with wooden picks.

2. While pork and tomatoes cook:
• Prepare orzo.

Menu
PointsPlus value
per serving: 10

Pork Tenderloin with Fig-Marsala Reduction

½ cup microwave mashed sweet potatoes
PointsPlus value
per serving: 3

1 cup steamed green beans
PointsPlus value
per serving: 0

Game Plan

1. While oven preheats:
• Season and brown pork.

2. While pork cooks:
• Steam beans.
• Prepare potatoes according to package directions.

3. While pork stands:
• Prepare fig-marsala reduction.

Pork Tenderloin with Fig-Marsala Reduction

prep: 4 minutes • **cook:** 29 minutes • **other:** 5 minutes
PointsPlus value per serving: 7

Garnish with quartered fresh figs if serving for company or a special occasion.

  1 (1-pound) pork tenderloin, trimmed
  ¼ teaspoon salt
  ¼ teaspoon freshly ground black pepper
  1 tablespoon olive oil
Cooking spray
  1 large shallot, minced
  ½ cup Marsala wine
  ¼ cup fig preserves

1. Preheat oven to 425°.
2. Sprinkle pork evenly with salt and pepper. Heat oil in a large nonstick skillet over medium-high heat. Add pork; cook 6 minutes or until browned on all sides.
3. Remove pork to a small roasting pan coated with cooking spray. Bake at 425° for 23 minutes or until thermometer registers 155° (slightly pink). Let stand 5 minutes; cut pork diagonally into thin slices.
4. While pork bakes, add shallots to pan. Sauté 2 minutes or until tender. Add Marsala and preserves; cook 3 minutes or until sauce thickens. Spoon sauce evenly over pork slices. Yield: 4 servings (serving size: 3 ounces pork and 2 tablespoons sauce).

Per serving: CALORIES 220; FAT 7.6g (sat 1.8g, mono 4g, poly 1g); PROTEIN 23.7g; CARB 12.7g; FIBER 0g; CHOL 74mg; IRON 1.3mg; SODIUM 208mg; CALC 12mg

Sweet-Spiced Grilled Lamb Chops

prep: 2 minutes • **cook:** 8 minutes   *PointsPlus* value per serving: 5

On cold days when you don't want to brave the outdoor grill, broil these lamb chops in the oven instead.

¾ teaspoon ground cinnamon
½ teaspoon freshly ground black pepper
¼ teaspoon ground allspice
¼ teaspoon ground cumin
⅛ teaspoon salt
⅛ teaspoon ground red pepper
8 (4-ounce) lamb loin chops, trimmed (about 1 inch thick)
Cooking spray
Lime wedges (optional)

1. Prepare grill.

2. Combine first 6 ingredients in a small bowl. Rub mixture evenly over lamb. Place lamb on grill rack coated with cooking spray. Grill 4 to 5 minutes on each side or until desired degree of doneness. Serve with lime wedges, if desired. **Yield:** 4 servings (serving size: 2 lamb chops).

Per serving: CALORIES 209; FAT 9g (sat 3.3g, mono 4.1g, poly 0.6g); PROTEIN 28.7g; CARB 0.7g; FIBER 0.4g; CHOL 90mg; IRON 2.1mg; SODIUM 153mg; CALC 26mg

Bulgur–Golden Raisin Pilaf

prep: 3 minutes • **cook:** 11 minutes • **other:** 2 minutes
PointsPlus value per serving: 5

1 cup water
½ cup bulgur wheat with soy grits hot cereal (such as Hodgson Mill)
½ cup golden raisins
¼ teaspoon crushed red pepper
¼ cup slivered almonds, toasted
2 teaspoons butter
¼ teaspoon salt

1. Combine first 4 ingredients in a medium saucepan; bring to a boil. Cover, reduce heat, and simmer 8 minutes or until water is almost absorbed.

2. Remove from heat; stir in remaining ingredients. Let stand, uncovered, 2 minutes. **Yield:** 4 servings (serving size: ½ cup).

Per serving: CALORIES 176; FAT 6g (sat 1.5g, mono 2.7g, poly 0.9g); PROTEIN 7.2g; CARB 28.8g; FIBER 3.2g; CHOL 5mg; IRON 1.6mg; SODIUM 161mg; CALC 49mg

---

Menu
PointsPlus value
per serving: 10

**Sweet-Spiced Grilled
Lamb Chops**

Bulgur–Golden Raisin Pilaf

Game Plan

1. While grill heats:
• Season lamb.
• Cook bulgur, raisins, and red pepper.

2. While lamb cooks:
• Combine remaining ingredients for pilaf, and let stand.

Menu

PointsPlus value
per serving: 12

Lamb Chops with Cherry Sauce

¹/₂ cup cooked couscous
PointsPlus value
per serving: 2

Game Plan

1. Season lamb.

2. While lamb cooks:
- Chop rosemary.
- Mince garlic.
- Prepare couscous
  according to package
  directions.

3. Prepare sauce.

Lamb Chops with Cherry Sauce

prep: 1 minute • **cook:** 14 minutes   *PointsPlus* value per serving: 10

Be sure to purchase lamb chops with an even thickness to ensure they all cook in the same amount of time.

  8 (4-ounce) lamb loin chops, trimmed (about ¾ inch thick)
  ¼ teaspoon salt
  ¼ teaspoon freshly ground black pepper
  Cooking spray
  2 garlic cloves, minced
  ¾ cup fat-free, lower-sodium beef broth
  ⅓ cup cherry preserves
  1 tablespoon chopped fresh rosemary
  2 tablespoons balsamic vinegar
  2 teaspoons cornstarch
  2 teaspoons water
  1 tablespoon butter
  Rosemary sprigs (optional)

1. Sprinkle lamb evenly with salt and pepper. Heat a large nonstick skillet over medium-high heat. Coat pan with cooking spray. Add lamb; cook 5 minutes on each side or until desired degree of doneness. Remove lamb from pan and keep warm.

2. Return pan to medium-high heat. Add garlic; cook 1 minute. Stir in beef broth and next 3 ingredients. Combine cornstarch and 2 teaspoons water; add to ingredients in pan. Cook 2 minutes or until thick. Add butter, stirring until butter melts. Spoon sauce evenly over lamb chops. Garnish with rosemary sprigs, if desired.

Yield: 4 servings (serving size: 2 lamb chops and ¼ cup sauce).

Per serving: CALORIES 401; FAT 16.2g (sat 6.5g, mono 6.5g, poly 1g); PROTEIN 40.9g; CARB 20.4g; FIBER 0.2g; CHOL 135mg; IRON 2.8mg; SODIUM 304mg; CALC 34mg

Poultry

pictured on page 114

Grilled Sun-Dried Tomato Chicken Breast

Menu
PointsPlus value
per serving: 6

Grilled Sun-Dried Tomato Chicken Breast

Warm Cannellini Bean Salad

Game Plan

1. While grill heats:
- Drain and rinse beans.
- Slice onion, and chop herbs.
- Combine pesto mixture.

2. While onion sautés:
- Grill chicken.

3. Add garlic, beans, peppers, and arugula to onion.

4. Top chicken with pesto mixture.

prep: 7 minutes • **cook:** 6 minutes   *PointsPlus* value per serving: 3

Chicken cutlets are a great convenience because they adapt to a variety of quick-cooking techniques, such as grilling, searing, and baking. Dress them up with bottled sun-dried tomato pesto embellished with fresh herbs and garlic.

2 tablespoons sun-dried tomato pesto (such as Classico)
2 tablespoons chopped fresh basil
1 tablespoon chopped fresh oregano
2 garlic cloves, minced
4 (4-ounce) chicken breast cutlets
¼ teaspoon salt
¼ teaspoon freshly ground black pepper
Cooking spray

1. Prepare grill.
2. Combine first 4 ingredients. Sprinkle chicken with salt and pepper; coat with cooking spray.
3. Place chicken on grill rack coated with cooking spray. Grill 3 minutes on each side or until done. Spoon pesto mixture evenly over chicken. **Yield:** 4 servings (serving size: 1 chicken cutlet and about 1 tablespoon pesto mixture).

Per serving: CALORIES 137; FAT 3.3g (sat 0.9g, mono 0.9g, poly 0.8g); PROTEIN 23.4g; CARB 1.8g; FIBER 0.2g; CHOL 63mg; IRON 1mg; SODIUM 279mg; CALC 21mg

Warm Cannellini Bean Salad

prep: 3 minutes • **cook:** 10 minutes   *PointsPlus* value per serving: 3

1 tablespoon olive oil
1 red onion, vertically cut into thin slices
3 garlic cloves, minced
1 (19-ounce) can cannellini beans, rinsed and drained
1 (12-ounce) bottle roasted red bell peppers
4 cups baby arugula
4 teaspoons balsamic glaze (such as Monari Federzoni)

1. Heat oil in a large nonstick skillet over medium heat. Add onion; cook 6 minutes or until lightly browned and tender, stirring occasionally.
2. Add garlic; sauté 1 minute. Add beans, peppers, and arugula; cook 1 to 2 minutes or just until arugula begins to wilt. Spoon salad evenly onto 4 plates. Drizzle with balsamic glaze. **Yield:** 4 servings (serving size: about 1 cup salad and 1 teaspoon glaze).

Per serving: CALORIES 134; FAT 3.9g (sat 0.5g, mono 2.5g, poly 0.7g); PROTEIN 4g; CARB 20.3g; FIBER 3.9g; CHOL 0mg; IRON 1.5mg; SODIUM 347mg; CALC 67mg

Cumin-Seared Chicken with Pineapple-Mint Salsa

prep: 1 minute • **cook:** 14 minutes   *PointsPlus* value per serving: 5

Buying refrigerated precubed pineapple makes it a breeze to put together this colorful salsa.

1	teaspoon ground cumin
½	teaspoon salt
⅛	teaspoon ground red pepper
4	(6-ounce) skinless, boneless chicken breast halves
	Cooking spray
1½	cups cubed pineapple, finely chopped
½	cup chopped fresh mint
¼	cup finely chopped red onion
2	tablespoons rice vinegar
2	teaspoons grated peeled fresh ginger

1. Combine cumin, salt, and red pepper; sprinkle evenly over chicken.
2. Heat a large nonstick skillet over medium-high heat. Coat pan with cooking spray. Add chicken; cook 7 to 8 minutes on each side or until done.
3. While chicken cooks, combine pineapple and next 4 ingredients; toss gently to blend. Serve with chicken. **Yield:** 4 servings (serving size: 1 chicken breast half and ½ cup salsa).

Per serving: CALORIES 224; FAT 2g (sat 0.6g, mono 0.5g, poly 0.5g); PROTEIN 39.9g; CARB 9.2g; FIBER 1.5g; CHOL 99mg; IRON 1.8mg; SODIUM 405mg; CALC 41mg

Almond-Coconut Rice

prep: 2 minutes • **cook:** 6 minutes   *PointsPlus* value per serving: 4

1	(10-ounce) package frozen whole-grain brown rice
⅓	cup slivered almonds
3	tablespoons flaked sweetened coconut
½	teaspoon ground cumin
⅛	teaspoon salt

1. Microwave rice according to package directions.
2. While rice cooks, heat a medium nonstick skillet over medium-high heat. Add almonds and coconut; cook 2 minutes or until lightly browned, stirring constantly. Remove from heat; add rice, cumin, and salt, stirring to blend. **Yield:** 4 servings (serving size: ¾ cup).

Per serving: CALORIES 147; FAT 6g (sat 1.4g, mono 3.1g, poly 1.3g); PROTEIN 4.2g; CARB 19.8g; FIBER 2.5g; CHOL 0mg; IRON 0.5mg; SODIUM 86mg; CALC 35mg

---

Menu
PointsPlus value
per serving: 9

Cumin-Seared Chicken with
Pineapple-Mint Salsa

Almond-Coconut Rice

Game Plan

1. Season chicken.

2. While chicken cooks:
  • Microwave rice.
  • Toast coconut and
    almonds.

3. Prepare pineapple-mint
salsa.

4. Add rice and seasonings to
coconut and almonds.

Menu
PointsPlus value
per serving: 7

Grilled Chicken with Rustic
Mustard Cream

Pan-Roasted Tomatoes with
Herbs

Game Plan

1. While grill heats:
- Season chicken.
- Chop herbs.

2. While chicken grills:
- Sauté tomatoes.
- Prepare mustard cream sauce.

3. Season tomatoes; let stand.

4. Combine chicken and sauce.

Grilled Chicken with Rustic Mustard Cream

prep: 6 minutes • **cook:** 12 minutes   *PointsPlus* value per serving: 6

The pronounced lemon-pine character of rosemary goes well with olive oil and Dijon mustard.

  1 tablespoon plus 1 teaspoon whole-grain Dijon mustard, divided
  1 tablespoon olive oil
  1 teaspoon chopped fresh rosemary
  ¼ teaspoon salt
  ¼ teaspoon black pepper
  4 (6-ounce) skinless, boneless chicken breast halves
Cooking spray
  3 tablespoons light mayonnaise
  1 tablespoon water
Rosemary sprigs (optional)

1. Prepare grill.

2. Combine 1 teaspoon mustard, oil, and next 3 ingredients in a small bowl; brush evenly over chicken. Place chicken on grill rack coated with cooking spray; grill 6 minutes on each side or until done.

3. While chicken grills, combine remaining 1 tablespoon mustard, mayonnaise, and 1 tablespoon water in a bowl. Serve mustard cream with grilled chicken. Garnish with rosemary sprigs, if desired. **Yield:** 4 servings (serving size: 1 chicken breast half and 1 tablespoon mustard cream).

Per serving: CALORIES 262; FAT 10g (sat 1.8g, mono 4g, poly 3g); PROTEIN 39.6g; CARB 1.7g; FIBER 0.2g; CHOL 102mg; IRON 1.4mg; SODIUM 448mg; CALC 25mg

Pan-Roasted Tomatoes with Herbs

prep: 2 minutes • **cook:** 4 minutes • **other:** 5 minutes
PointsPlus value per serving: 1

  2 teaspoons olive oil, divided
  1 pint multicolored grape tomatoes
  1 teaspoon chopped fresh oregano
  ½ teaspoon chopped fresh rosemary
  ¼ teaspoon salt
  ¼ teaspoon crushed red pepper

1. Heat 1 teaspoon oil in a medium nonstick skillet over medium-high heat. Add tomatoes; cook 3 to 4 minutes or until tomatoes begin to blister. Remove from heat; stir in remaining 1 teaspoon oil and remaining ingredients, tossing gently to combine. Let stand 5 minutes. **Yield:** 4 servings (serving size: ½ cup).

Per serving: CALORIES 34; FAT 3g (sat 0.4g, mono 1.7g, poly 0.4g); PROTEIN 0.7g; CARB 3.1g; FIBER 0.9g; CHOL 0mg; IRON 0.2mg; SODIUM 149mg; CALC 10mg

South-of-the-Border Grilled Chicken and Green Tomatoes

prep: 6 minutes • **cook:** 12 minutes • **other:** 30 minutes
PointsPlus value per serving: 7

The shortcut marinade begins with the flavorful drained liquid from the salsa. Choose a fresh juicy salsa with chunks of tomatoes and onions, which you can find in the deli or produce section of your supermarket, rather than a thick, tomato sauce–based product. Serve with tortillas.

1 (16-ounce) container fresh salsa
1 tablespoon olive oil
¼ teaspoon salt
¼ teaspoon black pepper
4 (6-ounce) skinless, boneless chicken breast halves
2 green tomatoes, each cut into 4 (½-inch-thick) slices
Cooking spray
½ cup (2 ounces) crumbled queso fresco

1. Drain salsa in a colander over a bowl, reserving liquid. Set salsa aside.
2. Combine reserved liquid, oil, salt, and pepper in a large zip-top plastic bag. Add chicken and tomato to bag; seal and shake gently to coat. Chill 30 minutes.
3. Prepare grill.
4. Remove chicken and tomato from bag, reserving marinade. Place chicken on grill rack coated with cooking spray; pour reserved marinade over chicken. Place tomato slices on grill rack. Grill chicken 6 minutes on each side or until done. Grill tomatoes 5 minutes on each side or until lightly browned. Serve chicken with tomatoes; top with reserved salsa and queso fresco. **Yield:** 4 servings (serving size: 2 tomato slices, 1 chicken breast half, about ½ cup salsa, and 2 tablespoons queso fresco).

Per serving: CALORIES 314; FAT 8g (sat 2.7g, mono 3.8g, poly 1.1g); PROTEIN 43.7g; CARB 8.7g; FIBER 0.7g; CHOL 109mg; IRON 1.7mg; SODIUM 588mg; CALC 115mg

---

Menu
PointsPlus value
per serving: 9

South-of-the-Border Grilled Chicken and Green Tomatoes

1 (6-inch) whole-wheat flour tortilla, warmed
PointsPlus value
per serving: 2

Game Plan

1. While chicken marinates:
• Prepare grill.

2. While chicken cooks:
• Slice and grill tomatoes.
• Warm tortillas on grill.

Menu
PointsPlus value
per serving: 11

Chicken and Shiitake Marsala

1 (6-ounce) baked potato with
2 teaspoons light butter
PointsPlus value
per serving: 4

1 cup steamed asparagus
PointsPlus value
per serving: 0

Game Plan

1. Pound and season chicken.

2. While chicken cooks:
• Chop green onions.
• Cook potato in micro-
  wave, and let stand.

3. After removing chicken:
• Prepare mushroom
  sauce.
• Steam asparagus.

Chicken and Shiitake Marsala

prep: 1 minute • **cook:** 14 minutes   *PointsPlus* value per serving: 7

Marsala, a fortified Italian wine recognized for its golden brown color and sweet, nutty flavor, is used in both sweet and savory dishes. Along with the smoky mushrooms in this recipe, the wine creates a rich, aromatic sauce. Dry sherry is a good substitute for Marsala.

 4 (6-ounce) skinless, boneless chicken breast halves
Cooking spray
¼ teaspoon salt
¼ teaspoon black pepper
 2 (3½-ounce) packages shiitake mushrooms, sliced
½ cup Marsala wine
 2 green onions, finely chopped (about ⅓ cup) and divided
 2 tablespoons butter

1. Place each chicken breast half between 2 sheets of heavy-duty plastic wrap; pound to ½-inch thickness using a meat mallet or small heavy skillet.

2. Heat a large nonstick skillet over medium-high heat. Coat pan with cooking spray. Sprinkle chicken evenly with salt and pepper. Add chicken to pan. Cook 5 to 6 minutes on each side or until done. Remove chicken and drippings from pan; set aside, and keep warm.

3. Heat pan over medium-high heat; coat pan with cooking spray. Add mushrooms. Coat mushrooms with cooking spray; cook 2 minutes or until tender, stirring frequently. Add wine and 3 tablespoons onions. Cook 30 seconds over high heat. Reduce heat; add butter, stirring until butter melts.

4. Add chicken and drippings to pan, stirring gently. Place chicken on a serving platter. Spoon mushroom sauce over chicken; sprinkle with remaining onions.

Yield: 4 servings (serving size: 1 chicken breast half and about ¼ cup mushroom sauce).

Per serving: CALORIES 291; FAT 8g (sat 4.2g, mono 2g, poly 0.7g); PROTEIN 40.9g; CARB 6.2g; FIBER 0.6g; CHOL 114mg; IRON 1.6mg; SODIUM 303mg; CALC 40mg

Roasted Chicken Breasts and Butternut Squash with Herbed Wine Sauce

prep: 9 minutes • **cook:** 45 minutes   *PointsPlus* value per serving: 10

Butternut squash's natural sugars caramelize during roasting. When paired with fines herbes and wine, they create a flavor explosion that rivals any bistro specialty.

     4   bone-in chicken breast halves (about 2 pounds), skinned
Cooking spray
     1   tablespoon olive oil, divided
     ½   teaspoon salt, divided
     ½   teaspoon freshly ground black pepper, divided
     5   cups (½-inch) cubed peeled butternut squash (2¼ pounds)
     1   teaspoon dried fines herbes
     3   tablespoons dry white wine

1. Preheat oven to 450°.
2. Place chicken in a large roasting pan coated with cooking spray. Brush chicken with 1½ teaspoons olive oil; sprinkle with ¼ teaspoon salt and ¼ teaspoon pepper.
3. Place squash in a large bowl. Drizzle with remaining 1½ teaspoons olive oil, and sprinkle with fines herbes, remaining ¼ teaspoon salt, and remaining ¼ teaspoon pepper; toss well. Add squash to pan. Bake at 450° for 38 minutes or until chicken is done. Transfer chicken and squash to a serving platter; keep warm.
4. Add wine to pan drippings; bring to a boil over high heat, scraping pan to loosen browned bits. Reduce heat; cook 2 minutes or until reduced to ¼ cup. Place 1 chicken breast half on each of 4 plates. Spoon 1 tablespoon sauce over each chicken breast. Serve with squash. **Yield:** 4 servings (serving size: 1 chicken breast half, 1 cup squash, and 1 tablespoon sauce).

Per serving: CALORIES 370; FAT 7.9g (sat 1.7g, mono 4g, poly 1.4g); PROTEIN 40.1g; CARB 36.5g; FIBER 6.1g; CHOL 102mg; IRON 3mg; SODIUM 539mg; CALC 164mg

Menu
PointsPlus value per serving: 10

Roasted Chicken Breast and Butternut Squash with Herbed Wine Sauce

1 cup salad greens with cucumber and fat-free vinaigrette
PointsPlus value per serving: 0

Game Plan

1. While oven preheats:
• Season chicken and squash.

2. While chicken and squash cook:
• Toss salad.

3. Prepare wine sauce.

pictured on page 113

Green Salsa Chicken

prep: 5 minutes • **cook:** 18 minutes   *PointsPlus* value per serving: 8

 1 lime
 4 tomatillos, husks and stems removed
 ¼ cup refrigerated prechopped tricolor bell pepper mix
 2 tablespoons chopped fresh cilantro
 2 (6-ounce) skinless, boneless chicken breast halves
 Cooking spray

1. Prepare grill.
2. Grate ⅛ teaspoon rind from lime, and squeeze juice to measure 1 tablespoon. Place rind and juice in a medium bowl. Cut tomatillos in half.
3. Heat a medium nonstick skillet over medium-high heat. Add tomatillo halves, skin sides down; cook 4 minutes or until lightly charred on edges. Turn tomatillos over, and move to 1 side of pan; add bell pepper to the other side. Cook 2 minutes or until bell pepper is lightly charred, stirring occasionally (do not stir tomatillos). Remove pan from heat; remove tomatillos from pan, and coarsely chop. Add tomatillo, bell pepper, and cilantro to lime juice mixture; toss well.
4. Place chicken on grill rack coated with cooking spray. Grill 6 minutes on each side or until done. Spoon tomatillo salsa over chicken. **Yield:** 2 servings (serving size: 1 chicken breast half and about ⅓ cup salsa).

Per serving: CALORIES 309; FAT 4.7g (sat 1.2g, mono 1.5g, poly 1.6g); PROTEIN 35g; CARB 31.1g; FIBER 2.3g; CHOL 94mg; IRON 1.6mg; SODIUM 437mg; CALC 22mg

Cumin Corn

prep: 5 minutes • **cook:** 10 minutes   *PointsPlus* value per serving: 3

 2 ears corn
 2 teaspoons butter
 ¼ cup finely chopped onion
 ¼ cup refrigerated prechopped tricolor bell pepper mix
 ¼ teaspoon ground cumin
 ⅛ teaspoon salt
 ⅛ teaspoon black pepper

1. Remove husks from corn; scrub silks from corn. Cut kernels from ears of corn; set corn aside. Discard cobs.
2. Melt butter in a nonstick skillet over medium heat. Add onion and bell pepper mix; cook, stirring constantly, 3 to 4 minutes or until crisp-tender. Stir in cumin, salt, and black pepper; cook 1 minute. Stir in corn; cook 5 minutes or until corn is crisp-tender, stirring frequently. **Yield:** 2 servings (serving size: ½ cup).

Per serving: CALORIES 122; FAT 5g (sat 2.6g, mono 1.3g, poly 0.7g); PROTEIN 3.3g; CARB 19.6g; FIBER 3.1g; CHOL 10mg; IRON 0.7mg; SODIUM 187mg; CALC 10mg

Balsamic Chicken with Roasted Tomatoes

prep: 5 minutes • **cook:** 12 minutes   *PointsPlus* value per serving: 5

- 1 pint grape tomatoes
- 1 tablespoon honey
- 1½ teaspoons olive oil
- ½ teaspoon salt, divided
- 4 (6-ounce) skinless, boneless chicken breast halves
- ½ teaspoon freshly ground black pepper
- Cooking spray
- Balsamic vinaigrette salad spritzer (such as Wish-Bone)

1. Preheat oven to 450°. Combine first 3 ingredients in a bowl; place tomato mixture on a foil-lined jelly-roll pan. Bake at 450° for 12 minutes or until tomato skins burst and begin to wrinkle, stirring once. Transfer tomatoes to a bowl, scraping juices into bowl. Stir ¼ teaspoon salt into tomato mixture. Place each breast half between 2 sheets of heavy-duty plastic wrap; pound to ¼-inch thickness using a meat mallet or small heavy skillet. Sprinkle chicken evenly with remaining ¼ teaspoon salt and ½ teaspoon pepper.

2. Heat a nonstick skillet over medium-high heat; coat with cooking spray. Add chicken; cook 3 to 4 minutes on each side. Coat each breast half with 2 to 3 sprays of balsamic spritzer. Spoon tomatoes evenly over chicken. **Yield:** 4 servings (serving size: 1 chicken breast half and about ¼ cup tomatoes).

Per serving: CALORIES 238; FAT 4g (sat 0.8g, mono 1.8g, poly 0.8g); PROTEIN 40g; CARB 7.7g; FIBER 1g; CHOL 99mg; IRON 1.5mg; SODIUM 431mg; CALC 28mg

Mushroom and Zucchini Orzo

prep: 6 minutes • **cook:** 12 minutes   *PointsPlus* value per serving: 5

- 1 cup uncooked orzo (rice-shaped pasta)
- Cooking spray
- 1 cup sliced mushrooms
- 1 cup diced zucchini
- 1 tablespoon butter
- ½ teaspoon dried oregano
- ¼ teaspoon salt
- ¼ teaspoon freshly ground black pepper

1. Cook orzo according to package directions, omitting salt and fat. Drain; keep warm. Heat a nonstick skillet over medium-high heat. Coat pan with cooking spray. Add mushrooms and zucchini; sauté 6 minutes. Combine orzo, mushroom mixture, and remaining ingredients in a large bowl, tossing gently. **Yield:** 4 servings (serving size: ¾ cup).

Per serving: CALORIES 197; FAT 4g (sat 1.8g, mono 0.7g, poly 0.1g); PROTEIN 6.3g; CARB 34.2g; FIBER 2.1g; CHOL 8mg; IRON 0.3mg; SODIUM 171mg; CALC 11mg

---

Menu
PointsPlus value
per serving: 10

Balsamic Chicken with Roasted Tomatoes

Mushroom and Zucchini Orzo

Game Plan

1. While oven preheats:
   - Prepare tomatoes for roasting.
   - Boil water for orzo.

2. While tomatoes cook:
   - Pound chicken.
   - Cook orzo.

3. While chicken cooks:
   - Sauté zucchini and mushrooms.

4. Prepare Mushroom and Zucchini Orzo.

Menu
PointsPlus value
per serving: 12

Mushroom-Herb Chicken

½ cup microwave mashed
potatoes
PointsPlus value
per serving: 4

1 cup steamed broccoli
PointsPlus value
per serving: 0

Game Plan

1. Pound and season chicken.

2. While chicken cooks:
  • Cut shallots.
  • Steam broccoli.

3. Sauté mushrooms and
shallots.

4. While chicken, mushrooms,
and shallots cook:
  • Prepare potatoes
    according to package
    directions.

Mushroom-Herb Chicken

prep: 5 minutes • **cook:** 14 minutes   *PointsPlus* value per serving: 8

Marjoram is oregano's mild cousin. Crush the dried leaves to release their delicate flavor. For this recipe, use the largest shallots you can find; three large shallots should yield 1 cup of slices. Refrigerated mashed potatoes and broccoli complete the meal.

> 4 (6-ounce) skinless, boneless chicken breast halves
> ¼ teaspoon salt
> ¼ teaspoon black pepper
> Cooking spray
> 3 large shallots, peeled
> 1 (8-ounce) package presliced mushrooms
> ⅓ cup dry sherry
> 1 teaspoon dried marjoram, crushed
> Freshly ground black pepper (optional)

1. Place each chicken breast half between 2 sheets of heavy-duty plastic wrap; pound to ⅓-inch thickness using a meat mallet or small heavy skillet. Sprinkle chicken evenly with salt and ¼ teaspoon pepper; coat with cooking spray. Heat a large nonstick skillet over medium-high heat. Add chicken to pan; cook 5 to 6 minutes on each side or until browned.

2. While chicken cooks, cut shallots vertically into thin slices. Remove chicken from pan. Coat pan with cooking spray. Add mushrooms and shallots to pan; coat vegetables with cooking spray. Cook 1 minute, stirring constantly. Stir in sherry and marjoram. Return chicken to pan; cover and cook 3 to 4 minutes or until mushrooms are tender and chicken is done. Transfer chicken to a serving platter. Pour mushroom mixture over chicken; sprinkle with freshly ground pepper, if desired. Serve immediately. **Yield:** 4 servings (serving size: 1 chicken breast half and ⅓ cup mushroom sauce).

Per serving: CALORIES 226; FAT 3g (sat 0.6g, mono 0.5g, poly 0.6g); PROTEIN 41.6g; CARB 5g; FIBER 1g; CHOL 99mg; IRON 1.9mg; SODIUM 262mg; CALC 33mg

Grilled Chicken with Tomato Chutney

prep: 2 minutes • **cook:** 10 minutes   *PointsPlus* value per serving: 6

Serve this Indian-inspired dish with grilled zucchini and couscous.

Cooking spray
½   cup chopped onion
1   teaspoon grated peeled fresh ginger
1   (14.5-ounce) can petite-cut diced tomatoes with garlic and olive oil, undrained
½   teaspoon salt, divided
¼   cup golden raisins
2   tablespoons chopped fresh cilantro
1   tablespoon brown sugar
¼   teaspoon ground cumin
4   (6-ounce) skinless, boneless chicken breast halves
¼   teaspoon freshly ground black pepper
Cilantro leaves (optional)

1. Prepare grill.

2. Heat a medium saucepan over medium-high heat. Coat pan with cooking spray. Add onion and ginger; sauté 3 minutes or until tender. Add tomatoes, ¼ teaspoon salt, and next 4 ingredients; bring to a boil. Cook 3 minutes or until thick, stirring occasionally.

3. While chutney cooks, sprinkle chicken evenly with remaining ¼ teaspoon salt and ¼ teaspoon pepper. Place chicken on grill rack coated with cooking spray; grill 4 minutes on each side or until done. Divide chicken among 4 plates. Spoon chutney over each chicken breast half, and garnish with cilantro leaves, if desired. **Yield:** 4 servings (serving size: 1 chicken breast half and ½ cup chutney).

Per serving: CALORIES 267; FAT 2.8g (sat 0.6g, mono 0.5g, poly 0.5g); PROTEIN 40.7g; CARB 19g; FIBER 1.6g; CHOL 106mg; IRON 1.5mg; SODIUM 771mg; CALC 32mg

---

Menu
PointsPlus value
per serving: 8

Grilled Chicken with Tomato
Chutney

½ cup cooked couscous
PointsPlus value
per serving: 2

1 cup grilled zucchini
PointsPlus value
per serving: 0

Game Plan

1. While grill heats:
• Sauté onion and ginger.

2. While chutney cooks:
• Grill chicken.
• Prepare couscous according to package directions.
• Grill zucchini.

Menu

PointsPlus value
per serving: 12

Moroccan-Spiced Chicken Thighs

1 cup steamed broccoli
PointsPlus value
per serving: 0

Whole-Wheat Couscous and Apricots

Game Plan

1. Season chicken.

2. While chicken and tomatoes cook:
• Prepare couscous.

3. While liquid reduces:
• Steam broccoli.

Moroccan-Spiced Chicken Thighs

prep: 8 minutes • **cook:** 15 minutes   *PointsPlus* value per serving: 7

Chicken thighs cooked in a smoky, acidic tomato sauce combine seamlessly with a sweet, nutty couscous to create a hearty North African–inspired meal. While the chicken simmers, prepare the couscous so both dishes will be ready at the same time.

½ teaspoon smoked paprika
½ teaspoon ground cumin
½ teaspoon dried thyme
¼ teaspoon salt
8 skinless, boneless chicken thighs (about 1½ pounds)
Cooking spray
1 (14.5-ounce) can fire-roasted diced tomatoes with garlic, undrained
Chopped fresh cilantro (optional)

1. Combine first 4 ingredients. Rub chicken thighs with spice mixture.
2. Heat a large nonstick skillet over medium-high heat. Coat pan with cooking spray. Add chicken; cook 2 minutes. Turn chicken over; stir in tomatoes. Bring to a boil; cover, reduce heat, and simmer 10 minutes. Uncover and cook 1 minute or until liquid is reduced by half. Sprinkle with cilantro, if desired. Yield: 4 servings (serving size: 2 chicken thighs and ¼ cup tomato sauce).

Per serving: CALORIES 273; FAT 12.9g (sat 3.6g, mono 4.9g, poly 3.6g); PROTEIN 31.4g; CARB 5.4g; FIBER 1.2g; CHOL 112mg; IRON 3mg; SODIUM 479mg; CALC 42mg

Whole-Wheat Couscous and Apricots

prep: 5 minutes • **cook:** 5 minutes • **other:** 5 minutes
PointsPlus value per serving: 5

2 teaspoons olive oil
¾ cup whole-wheat couscous
1 cup fat-free, lower-sodium chicken broth
⅓ cup diced dried apricots
⅓ cup slivered almonds, toasted

1. Heat oil in a medium saucepan over medium heat. Add couscous; sauté 1 minute. Stir in broth and apricots. Bring to a boil; remove from heat. Let stand 5 minutes or until liquid is absorbed. Add almonds; fluff with a fork. Yield: 4 servings (serving size: about ⅔ cup).

Per serving: CALORIES 196; FAT 7.6g (sat 0.8g, mono 4.7g, poly 1.4g); PROTEIN 6.6g; CARB 27.7g; FIBER 4.4g; CHOL 0mg; IRON 1.7mg; SODIUM 19mg; CALC 39mg

Chicken Thighs with Orange-Ginger Glaze

prep: 1 minute • **cook:** 14 minutes   *PointsPlus* value per serving: 8

    8   skinless, boneless chicken thighs (about 1½ pounds)
    ½   teaspoon salt
    ¼   teaspoon black pepper
    ⅛   teaspoon garlic powder
  1½   teaspoons olive oil
    1   navel orange
    3   tablespoons honey
    1   teaspoon grated peeled fresh ginger

1. Sprinkle chicken with salt, pepper, and garlic powder. Heat oil in a large nonstick skillet over medium-high heat. Add chicken; cook 3 to 4 minutes on each side or until browned.

2. While chicken cooks, grate 1 teaspoon rind from orange, and squeeze juice to measure ¼ cup. Add orange rind, juice, honey, and ginger to chicken, scraping to loosen browned bits. Bring to a boil; reduce heat, and simmer, uncovered, 7 minutes or until chicken is done and orange mixture is syrupy. **Yield:** 4 servings (serving size: 2 chicken thighs and about 1½ tablespoons sauce).

Per serving: CALORIES 327; FAT 14.5g (sat 3.8g, mono 6.4g, poly 3.6g); PROTEIN 30.9g; CARB 17.7g; FIBER 0.9g; CHOL 112mg; IRON 1.7mg; SODIUM 395mg; CALC 31mg

Menu

PointsPlus value per serving: 14

Chicken Thighs with Orange-Ginger Glaze

½ cup precooked white rice
PointsPlus value per serving: 3

Roasted Broccoli with Almonds

Game Plan

1. While oven preheats:
   • Cut and season broccoli.
   • Season chicken.

2. While broccoli and chicken cook:
   • Grate and juice orange.
   • Toast almonds.

3. Simmer sauce for chicken.

4. Heat rice.

Roasted Broccoli with Almonds

prep: 6 minutes • **cook:** 14 minutes   *PointsPlus* value per serving: 3

  1¼   pounds fresh broccoli crowns (about 3)
       Cooking spray
    1   tablespoon olive oil
    1   garlic clove, pressed
    ¼   teaspoon salt
    ¼   teaspoon black pepper
    3   tablespoons sliced almonds

1. Preheat oven to 475°.

2. Cut broccoli into 3-inch-long spears; cut thick stems in half lengthwise. Place broccoli in a single layer on a jelly-roll pan coated with cooking spray.

3. Combine olive oil and garlic; drizzle broccoli with oil mixture, and toss well. Sprinkle with salt and pepper. Bake at 475° for 14 minutes (do not stir).

4. While broccoli roasts, cook almonds, stirring constantly, in a small skillet over medium heat 2 minutes or until toasted. Sprinkle roasted broccoli with toasted almonds. **Yield:** 4 servings (serving size: about 1 cup).

Per serving: CALORIES 97; FAT 6.1g (sat 0.7g, mono 3.9g, poly 1.1g); PROTEIN 5.2g; CARB 8.6g; FIBER 4.8g; CHOL 0mg; IRON 1.5mg; SODIUM 184mg; CALC 81mg

pictured on page 48

Grilled Asian Drumsticks

prep: 4 minutes • **cook:** 20 minutes   ***PointsPlus*** value per serving: 5

These drumsticks are a perfect balance of smoky, sweet, and spicy.

> 8   chicken drumsticks (about 2 pounds), skinned
> Cooking spray
> 3   tablespoons balsamic vinegar
> 3   tablespoons lower-sodium soy sauce
> 3   tablespoons honey
> 2   teaspoons chile paste with garlic (such as sambal oelek)

1. Prepare grill.

2. Coat chicken and grill rack with cooking spray. Grill chicken 20 minutes or until done, turning once.

3. While chicken grills, combine vinegar and next 3 ingredients in a medium saucepan, stirring with a whisk. Bring to a boil; cook 4 minutes or until reduced to ⅓ cup.

4. Transfer chicken to a large bowl or pan. Pour sauce over chicken, turning to coat. **Yield:** 4 servings (serving size: 2 drumsticks and about 3 tablespoons sauce).

Per serving: CALORIES 210; FAT 4g (sat 1.1g, mono 1.4g, poly 1.1g); PROTEIN 26.3g; CARB 15.6g; FIBER 0g; CHOL 98mg; IRON 1.5mg; SODIUM 855mg; CALC 18mg

Spicy-Sweet Broccoli

prep: 3 minutes • **cook:** 4 minutes   ***PointsPlus*** value per serving: 2

> 1   (12-ounce) package refrigerated broccoli florets
> 2   tablespoons lower-sodium soy sauce
> 2   tablespoons rice vinegar
> 1   tablespoon dark sesame oil
> 2   teaspoons sugar
> ¼   teaspoon crushed red pepper

1. Microwave broccoli according to package directions. Drain. Combine soy sauce and next 4 ingredients in a small bowl. Drizzle over cooked broccoli. **Yield:** 4 servings (serving size: ¾ cup).

Per serving: CALORIES 62; FAT 4g (sat 0.6g, mono 1.4g, poly 1.7g); PROTEIN 2.6g; CARB 6.6g; FIBER 2.5g; CHOL 0mg; IRON 0.8mg; SODIUM 473mg; CALC 41mg

---

Menu
PointsPlus value
per serving: 11

Grilled Asian Drumsticks

1 (6-inch) baked sweet potato
with 2 teaspoons light butter
PointsPlus value
per serving: 4

Spicy-Sweet Broccoli

Game Plan

1. While grill heats:
• Microwave sweet potato, and let stand.

2. While chicken grills:
• Microwave broccoli.
• Boil sauce for chicken.
• Combine dressing for broccoli.

3. Combine chicken and sauce; combine broccoli and dressing.

Southwest Barbecue Chicken Pizza

prep: 5 minutes • **cook:** 17 minutes   *PointsPlus* value per serving: 9

For a smokier flavor, use pulled smoked chicken from your favorite barbecue restaurant. Find fresh pizza dough in the bakery section of some grocery stores, or stop by your favorite pizza joint.

1   (16-ounce) portion fresh pizza dough
Olive oil–flavored cooking spray
½   cup barbecue sauce
2   cups shredded cooked chicken
1   cup frozen whole-kernel corn, thawed
1   cup (4 ounces) preshredded reduced-fat Mexican blend cheese
½   cup sliced green onions (optional)

1. Preheat oven to 450°. Place a large baking sheet on bottom rack in oven while it preheats.

2. Roll dough into a 12-inch circle on a lightly floured surface. Coat preheated baking sheet with cooking spray. Slide dough onto baking sheet.

3. Spread barbecue sauce evenly over dough. Top evenly with chicken, corn, and cheese. Bake at 450° for 17 minutes or until crust is golden brown and cheese melts. Sprinkle with green onions, if desired, just before serving. Cut pizza into 12 wedges. **Yield:** 6 servings (serving size: 2 wedges).

Per serving: CALORIES 361; FAT 7.2g (sat 2.5g, mono 0.7g, poly 0.5g); PROTEIN 27.2g; CARB 45.8g; FIBER 2.1g; CHOL 46mg; IRON 2.6mg; SODIUM 705mg; CALC 146mg

Menu
PointsPlus value
per serving: 9

Southwest Barbecue
Chicken Pizza

1 cup mixed baby greens with
fat-free vinaigrette
PointsPlus value
per serving: 0

Game Plan

1. While oven preheats:
• Roll pizza dough.
• Assemble pizza.

2. While pizza cooks:
• Toss salad.

Game Plan

1. While pasta cooks:
  • Season and sauté
    chicken.

2. Sauté vegetables.

3. Drain pasta, and combine
  with chicken mixture.

Sun-Dried Tomato–Pesto Chicken Pasta

prep: 2 minutes • **cook:** 13 minutes   *PointsPlus* value per serving: 10

We chose chicken cutlets for this recipe because they are thin and cook quickly. Any boneless chicken breast will work, though.

2	cups multigrain rotini pasta (such as Barilla PLUS)
4	(4-ounce) chicken breast cutlets, cubed
¼	teaspoon salt
¼	teaspoon black pepper
2	teaspoons olive oil
2	medium zucchini, halved lengthwise and cut into slices
1	(8-ounce) container refrigerated prechopped onion
1½	cups spicy red pepper pasta sauce (such as Classico)
¼	cup sun-dried tomato pesto (such as Classico)
6	tablespoons (1.5 ounces) shredded fresh Parmesan cheese

1. Cook pasta according to package directions, omitting salt and fat.

2. While pasta cooks, sprinkle chicken with salt and pepper. Heat oil in a large nonstick skillet over medium-high heat. Add chicken to pan. Sauté 3 minutes or until browned. Add zucchini and onion; sauté 6 minutes or until vegetables are crisp-tender and chicken is done.

3. Add pasta sauce and pesto to pan; cook 2 minutes or until thoroughly heated. Drain pasta, and immediately add to pan, tossing well. Divide evenly among 6 plates; sprinkle each serving with Parmesan cheese. **Yield:** 6 servings (serving size: 1⅓ cups chicken mixture and 1 tablespoon Parmesan cheese).

Per serving: CALORIES 382; FAT 11.8g (sat 3.8g, mono 3.6g, poly 0.8g); PROTEIN 31.8g; CARB 37g; FIBER 5.2g; CHOL 56mg; IRON 3.2mg; SODIUM 643mg; CALC 224mg

Turkey-Basil Rolls

prep: 10 minutes • **cook:** 5 minutes   *PointsPlus* **value per serving: 7**

Cooking spray
¾ pound ground turkey
½ teaspoon salt-free Thai seasoning blend (such as Frontier)
¼ teaspoon freshly ground black pepper
⅛ teaspoon salt
¾ cup cabbage-and-carrot coleslaw
6 (8-inch) round sheets rice paper
12 basil leaves
6 tablespoons light sesame-ginger dressing (such as Newman's Own)

1. Heat a large nonstick skillet over medium-high heat. Coat pan with cooking spray. Add turkey and next 3 ingredients; cook 5 minutes or until done. Combine turkey mixture and coleslaw in a medium bowl.
2. Add hot water to a large, shallow dish to a depth of 1 inch. Place 1 rice paper sheet in dish; let stand 30 seconds or just until soft. Place sheet on a flat surface. Arrange 2 basil leaves on top third of sheet. Arrange ⅓ cup turkey mixture on bottom third of sheet. Folding sides of sheet over filling and starting with filled side, roll up jelly-roll fashion. Gently press seam to seal. Place roll, seam side down, on a serving platter (cover to keep from drying).
3. Repeat procedure with remaining sheets, basil, and turkey mixture. Slice each roll in half diagonally. Serve rolls with dressing as a dipping sauce. **Yield:** 3 servings (serving size: 2 rolls and 2 tablespoons dipping sauce).

Per serving: CALORIES 263; FAT 9g (sat 2g, mono 4.5g, poly 2.3g); PROTEIN 24.5g; CARB 20.8g; FIBER 0.4g; CHOL 65mg; IRON 2.3mg; SODIUM 589mg; CALC 9mg

> **Menu**
> *PointsPlus* value
> per serving: 13
>
> **Turkey-Basil Rolls**
>
> **Mandarin Oranges with Grand Marnier and Mascarpone**
>
> ### Game Plan
>
> **1.** While turkey, seasonings, and cabbage cook:
> • Prepare Mandarin Oranges with Grand Marnier and Mascarpone.
>
> **2.** Soften rice wrappers, and assemble rolls.

Mandarin Oranges with Grand Marnier and Mascarpone

prep: 8 minutes   *PointsPlus* **value per serving: 6**

¼ cup reduced-fat sour cream
2 tablespoons mascarpone cheese
4 teaspoons sugar
1 (15-ounce) can mandarin oranges in light syrup, drained
1½ tablespoons Grand Marnier (orange-flavored liqueur)
Mint leaves (optional)

1. Combine first 3 ingredients in a small bowl, stirring with a whisk until sugar dissolves.
2. Combine oranges and liqueur; spoon evenly into 3 wine glasses or dessert dishes. Spoon sour cream mixture over oranges; garnish with mint leaves, if desired. **Yield:** 3 servings (serving size: about 2½ tablespoons oranges and 1 tablespoon sour cream topping).

Per serving: CALORIES 200; FAT 11g (sat 6.2g, mono 0g, poly 0g); PROTEIN 3g; CARB 19.9g; FIBER 0.8g; CHOL 34mg; IRON 0.3mg; SODIUM 28mg; CALC 72mg

Menu
PointsPlus value
per serving: 6

Smoked Sausage and Corn
Frittata

Sweet Lemon-Splashed Melon

Game Plan

1. While sausage and corn cook:
   • Combine eggs.

2. Add eggs to pan, and cover.

3. While eggs cook:
   • Prepare melon.

Smoked Sausage and Corn Frittata

prep: 3 minutes • **cook:** 16 minutes • **other:** 2 minutes
PointsPlus value per serving: 4

Browning intensifies the smokiness of the sausage, allowing you to use less sausage while achieving maximum results in this simple-to-prepare frittata.

Cooking spray
4 ounces smoked turkey sausage, quartered lengthwise and diced
1½ cups frozen shoepeg white corn, thawed
¼ teaspoon ground red pepper (optional)
1 large egg
4 large egg whites
½ cup (2 ounces) reduced-fat shredded sharp cheddar cheese
3 tablespoons chopped fresh cilantro, divided

1. Heat a medium nonstick skillet over medium-high heat. Coat pan with cooking spray. Add sausage; sauté 4 minutes or until browned. Stir in corn and, if desired, red pepper; reduce heat to medium-low.
2. Combine egg and egg whites in a small bowl; stir with a whisk. Drizzle evenly over sausage mixture. Cover and cook 8 minutes or until almost set. Remove pan from heat; sprinkle evenly with cheese and 1½ tablespoons cilantro. Cover and let stand 2 minutes. Sprinkle with remaining 1½ tablespoons cilantro. Cut into 4 wedges. **Yield:** 4 servings (serving size: 1 wedge).

Per serving: CALORIES 174; FAT 6g (sat 2.9g, mono 0.5g, poly 0.2g); PROTEIN 13.8g; CARB 14.5g; FIBER 1.6g; CHOL 76mg; IRON 0.6mg; SODIUM 472mg; CALC 121mg

Sweet Lemon-Splashed Melon

prep: 3 minutes   *PointsPlus* value per serving: 2

3 cups cubed peeled cantaloupe
1 tablespoon sugar
½ teaspoon grated lemon rind
1 tablespoon fresh lemon juice

1. Combine all ingredients in a medium bowl; toss gently to coat. **Yield:** 4 servings (serving size: ¾ cup).

Per serving: CALORIES 54; FAT 0g (sat 0.1g, mono 0g, poly 0.1g); PROTEIN 1g; CARB 13.3g; FIBER 0g; CHOL 0mg; IRON 0.3mg; SODIUM 19mg; CALC 11mg

Salads

Menu
PointsPlus value
per serving: 12

Whole-Wheat Mediterranean
Panzanella

Prosciutto-Wrapped
Melon Slices

Game Plan

1. Chop tomato, cucumber, and basil.

2. Assemble Prosciutto-Wrapped Melon Slices.

3. Combine dressing.

4. Toss panzanella.

Whole-Wheat Mediterranean Panzanella

prep: 10 minutes   *PointsPlus* value per serving: 10

Like many Italian dishes, panzanella (pahn-zah-NEHL-lah) was probably first made out of necessity—combining stale bread with readily available fresh garden vegetables. This classic bread salad, full of juicy tomatoes, is like summer on a plate. For added color, we chose to use a combination of yellow and red heirloom tomatoes. If you prefer a drier panzanella, toast the bread before tossing it with the tomato mixture.

       3   tablespoons white balsamic vinegar
       1   tablespoon vegetable oil
       ¼   teaspoon black pepper
       ⅛   teaspoon salt
    6½   cups chopped tomato (3 very large)
    1½   cups cubed English cucumber
       ½   cup pitted kalamata olives
       ½   cup fresh basil leaves, torn
       6   ounces whole-wheat country-style bread, torn into bite-sized pieces (4 cups)
       1   (4-ounce) package crumbled feta cheese

1. Combine first 4 ingredients in a large bowl, stirring with a whisk. Stir in tomato and next 3 ingredients. Add bread and cheese; toss gently. Serve immediately. **Yield:** 4 servings (serving size: about 2⅔ cups).

Per serving: CALORIES 362; FAT 20.4g (sat 5.7g, mono 9.2g, poly 4.2g); PROTEIN 13.7g; CARB 36.7g; FIBER 8.7g; CHOL 25mg; IRON 3.1mg; SODIUM 898mg; CALC 241mg

Prosciutto-Wrapped Melon Slices

prep: 8 minutes   *PointsPlus* value per serving: 2

       1   small cantaloupe, peeled, seeded, and cut into 8 wedges
       4   ounces thinly sliced prosciutto

1. Wrap melon wedges evenly with prosciutto. **Yield:** 4 servings (serving size: 2 wedges).

Per serving: CALORIES 88; FAT 2.8g (sat 0.9g, mono 1.3g, poly 0.5g); PROTEIN 7.3g; CARB 9g; FIBER 0g; CHOL 17mg; IRON 0.6mg; SODIUM 443mg; CALC 12mg

Yucatecan Rice Salad

prep: 7 minutes • **cook:** 7 minutes • **other:** 5 minutes
PointsPlus value per serving: 5

Yucatecan cuisine combines Spanish, Mexican, and Caribbean flavors. In this spicy recipe, an authentic combination of turmeric, black beans, and olives accompanies the rice. Serve with lemon wedges, if desired.

- ½ cup water
- ⅛ teaspoon ground turmeric
- ½ cup instant whole-grain brown rice (such as Minute)
- 1 (15-ounce) can black beans, rinsed and drained
- ½ cup jalapeño-stuffed green olives, coarsely chopped (about 11 olives)
- ⅓ cup prechopped red onion
- 3 (0.5-ounce) slices reduced-fat Monterey Jack cheese with jalapeño peppers, cut into ½-inch squares
- ¼ cup chopped fresh cilantro
- 1 tablespoon extra-virgin olive oil
- Lemon wedges (optional)

1. Bring ½ cup water and turmeric to a boil in a medium saucepan. Stir in rice; cover, reduce heat, and simmer 5 minutes. Remove from heat. Place rice in a wire mesh strainer; rinse rice with cold water, and drain well.

2. While rice cooks, combine beans and next 5 ingredients in a medium bowl. Add cooled rice; toss gently until blended. Serve with lemon wedges, if desired. **Yield:** 4 servings (serving size: ¾ cup).

Per serving: CALORIES 164; FAT 8.3g (sat 1.8g, mono 4.9g, poly 1.3g); PROTEIN 6.4g; CARB 20.9g; FIBER 4.1g; CHOL 8mg; IRON 1.2mg; SODIUM 430mg; CALC 102mg

Menu

PointsPlus value per serving: 9

Yucatecan Rice Salad

Tomato-Avocado Wedges

Game Plan

1. While water and turmeric come to a boil:
- Chop olives and cilantro.
- Slice tomatoes and avocado.

2. While rice cooks:
- Combine remaining ingredients for rice salad.
- Assemble Tomato-Avocado Wedges.

3. Rinse rice, and top salad.

Tomato-Avocado Wedges

prep: 4 minutes   *PointsPlus* value per serving: 4

- 2 medium tomatoes, each cut into 8 wedges
- 1 medium avocado, thinly sliced
- 1½ tablespoons extra-virgin olive oil
- 1½ tablespoons cider vinegar
- ⅛ teaspoon salt
- 1 garlic clove, minced

1. Combine tomato and avocado in a medium bowl.

2. Combine olive oil and next 3 ingredients in a small bowl, stirring with a whisk. Drizzle dressing over tomato mixture. **Yield:** 4 servings (serving size: ½ cup).

Per serving: CALORIES 135; FAT 11.9g (sat 1.5g, mono 9g, poly 1.4g); PROTEIN 2.1g; CARB 7.5g; FIBER 2.4g; CHOL 0mg; IRON 0.7mg; SODIUM 77mg; CALC 9mg

Menu

PointsPlus value
per serving: 8

Couscous, Sweet Potato, and
Black Soybean Salad

1 (6-inch) whole-wheat pita,
quartered and toasted
PointsPlus value
per serving: 2

Game Plan

1. While water for couscous
comes to a boil:
- Rinse and drain black
beans.
- Rinse spinach.

2. While couscous stands:
- Microwave sweet potato.
- Combine remaining
ingredients.

3. Assemble salad.

Couscous, Sweet Potato, and Black Soybean Salad

prep: 5 minutes • **cook:** 5 minutes • **other:** 5 minutes
PointsPlus value per serving: 6

Choose this lime-basil–infused salad—with chunks of beta-carotene–laced sweet potatoes and tender, high-fiber, protein-rich black soybeans—for a healthy meatless main dish you can have on the table in 15 minutes.

¾   cup water
⅔   cup wheat couscous
1   (16-ounce) package refrigerated cubed peeled sweet potato (such as Glory)
¼   cup fat-free lime-basil vinaigrette (such as Maple Grove Farms)
½   teaspoon freshly ground black pepper
¼   teaspoon salt
1   (15-ounce) can no-salt-added black soybeans (such as Eden Organic), rinsed and drained
2   cups baby spinach
5   tablespoons crumbled reduced-fat feta cheese
3   green onions, chopped

1. Bring ¾ cup water to a boil in a medium saucepan; gradually stir in couscous. Remove from heat; cover and let stand 5 minutes. Fluff with a fork.
2. While couscous stands, place sweet potato on a microwave-safe plate. Microwave at HIGH 5 minutes or until tender.
3. Combine vinaigrette, pepper, and salt in a large bowl; stir well with a whisk. Add couscous, sweet potato, soybeans, and spinach; toss gently to coat. Top each serving with cheese; sprinkle evenly with onions. **Yield:** 5 servings (serving size: about 1⅓ cups couscous salad and 1 tablespoon cheese).

Per serving: CALORIES 228; FAT 4g (sat 1.1g, mono 0.7g, poly 1.7g); PROTEIN 10.5g; CARB 39.8g; FIBER 7.3g; CHOL 3mg; IRON 2.4mg; SODIUM 287mg; CALC 102mg

Grilled Pesto Salmon–Orzo Salad

prep: 9 minutes • **cook:** 14 minutes

PointsPlus value per serving: 7

  2 (6-ounce) skinless salmon fillets
  ¼ cup commercial pesto, divided
  ¼ teaspoon kosher salt
  ¼ teaspoon freshly ground black pepper
  2 (½-inch-thick) slices sweet onion
1½ cups grape tomatoes
    Cooking spray
    Orzo with Arugula and White Beans
  ⅛ teaspoon freshly ground black pepper

1. Prepare grill.

2. Brush fish evenly with 2 tablespoons pesto; sprinkle with salt and ¼ teaspoon pepper. Brush 1 tablespoon pesto over onion slices. Toss tomatoes with remaining 1 tablespoon pesto, and place on a 12-inch square of heavy-duty foil. Fold edges of foil up around tomatoes to form a bowl, keeping tomatoes in a single layer (do not completely enclose).

3. Place fish, onion slices, and foil bowl with tomatoes on grill rack coated with cooking spray. Grill 14 minutes or until fish is desired degree of doneness, onion is tender, and tomatoes begin to burst, turning fish and onion after 7 minutes.

4. Using a fork, gently break fish into large chunks, and chop onion slices. Combine Orzo with Arugula and White Beans, fish, onion, tomatoes, and accumulated tomato juice. Toss gently; sprinkle with ⅛ teaspoon pepper. **Yield:** 6 servings (serving size: 1½ cups).

Per serving: CALORIES 279; FAT 8.4g (sat 1.5g, mono 3.6g, poly 2.3g); PROTEIN 36.6g; CARB 12.4g; FIBER 2.5g; CHOL 89mg; IRON 2mg; SODIUM 673mg; CALC 51mg

---

Menu
PointsPlus value per serving: 7

Grilled Pesto Salmon–Orzo Salad

Orzo with Arugula and White Beans

Game Plan

1. While grill heats:
• Slice onions.
• Prepare salmon fillets.
• Boil water for orzo.

2. While salmon grills:
• Cook and drain orzo.
• Combine orzo with arugula and white beans.

3. Assemble salad.

Orzo with Arugula and White Beans

prep: 13 minutes • **cook:** 11 minutes

PointsPlus value per serving: 3

  1 cup uncooked orzo (rice-shaped pasta)
  1 (15.5-ounce) can cannellini beans, rinsed and drained
  2 cups firmly packed arugula
  2 tablespoons fresh lemon juice

1. Cook orzo according to package directions, omitting salt and fat. Drain.

2. Combine orzo, beans, arugula, and lemon juice in a large bowl. **Yield:** 6 servings (serving size: 1 cup).

Per serving: CALORIES 140; FAT 0.7g (sat 0g, mono 0g, poly 0.2g); PROTEIN 5.3g; CARB 27.5g; FIBER 2.7g; CHOL 0mg; IRON 0.7mg; SODIUM 85mg; CALC 24mg

Game Plan

1. While oven preheats:
  • Split pitas, and place on baking sheet.
  • Drain and chop artichoke hearts.

2. While pitas bake:
  • Assemble salad.

Tuna, Artichoke, and Roasted Red Bell Pepper Salad

prep: 9 minutes   *PointsPlus* value per serving: 4

A medley of Mediterranean flavors perks up humble albacore tuna in this no-cook dish. It can be made ahead for a lunch-to-go or prepared for dinner. Just add the spinach and toss before serving. For sandwich variations, stuff the tuna mixture into whole-wheat pita halves, or spread it between two baguette halves.

  1   (12-ounce) jar marinated quartered artichoke hearts (such as Reese)
  ¼   cup chopped fresh dill
  1   tablespoon extra-virgin olive oil
  1   tablespoon fresh lemon juice
  ½   teaspoon freshly ground black pepper
  2   garlic cloves, minced
  2   cups chopped bagged fresh baby spinach
  2   (5-ounce) cans albacore tuna in water, drained and flaked
  1   (12-ounce) bottle roasted red bell peppers, drained and chopped

1. Drain artichokes, reserving 2 tablespoons marinade. Coarsely chop artichokes. Combine artichokes, reserved marinade, dill, and next 4 ingredients in a large bowl. Add spinach, tuna, and roasted bell peppers, tossing well. Yield: 4 servings (serving size: 1¼ cups).

Per serving: CALORIES 153; FAT 6.8g (sat 0.5g, mono 3g, poly 2.7g); PROTEIN 15.1g; CARB 9.3g; FIBER 2.2g; CHOL 23mg; IRON 0.7mg; SODIUM 468mg; CALC 17mg

Feta Pita Crisps

prep: 4 minutes • **cook:** 10 minutes   *PointsPlus* value per serving: 5

  3   (6-inch) pitas
  1   (3.5-ounce) package crumbled reduced-fat feta cheese, finely chopped
Olive oil–flavored cooking spray

1. Preheat oven to 425°.
2. Split pitas; cut each into 6 wedges. Arrange pita wedges in a single layer on a large baking sheet; sprinkle with cheese, and lightly coat with cooking spray.
3. Bake at 425° for 10 minutes or until crisp and golden. Yield: 4 servings (serving size: 9 pita crisps).

Per serving: CALORIES 173; FAT 3.5g (sat 2.2g, mono 0.9g, poly 0.1g); PROTEIN 10.4g; CARB 25.5g; FIBER 1.1g; CHOL 7mg; IRON 2mg; SODIUM 463mg; CALC 103mg

pictured on page 117

Grilled Southwestern Shrimp Salad with Lime-Cumin Dressing

prep: 2 minutes • **cook:** 12 minutes   *PointsPlus* value per serving: 7

We tested this recipe with peeled and deveined shrimp. Whether you have your fishmonger peel and devein them or you do it yourself, you'll need to start with 1 pound of unpeeled shrimp.

¾ pound peeled and deveined large shrimp
1 teaspoon chili powder
2 ears corn
Cooking spray
6 cups chopped romaine lettuce
2 large tomatoes, cut into 8 wedges
Lime-Cumin Dressing
1 cup diced peeled avocado (1 small)

1. Prepare grill.

2. Sprinkle shrimp evenly with chili powder. Remove husks from corn; scrub silks from corn. Place corn on grill rack coated with cooking spray. Grill 12 minutes, turning occasionally. Add shrimp to grill rack after 6 minutes; grill 3 minutes on each side. Cut kernels from ears of corn. Discard cobs.

3. Combine shrimp, corn, lettuce, and tomato in a large bowl; drizzle with Lime-Cumin Dressing, and toss well. Add avocado; toss gently. Serve immediately. **Yield:** 4 servings (serving size: 3¼ cups).

Per serving: CALORIES 266; FAT 11.2g (sat 1.5g, mono 5.7g, poly 2.7g); PROTEIN 21.4g; CARB 24g; FIBER 5.9g; CHOL 129mg; IRON 3.8mg; SODIUM 404mg; CALC 90mg

Menu

PointsPlus value
per serving: 7

Grilled Southwestern Shrimp Salad with Lime-Cumin Dressing

Game Plan

1. While grill heats:
 • Season shrimp.
 • Shuck and clean corn.

2. While corn grills:
 • Combine dressing.
 • Cut tomato and lettuce.

3. While shrimp cook:
 • Dice avocado.
 • Combine dressing.

4. Assemble salad.

Lime-Cumin Dressing

prep: 4 minutes   *PointsPlus* value per serving: 2

¼ cup fresh lime juice
1 tablespoon canola oil
1 tablespoon honey
½ teaspoon kosher salt
½ teaspoon ground cumin
⅛ teaspoon coarsely ground black pepper

1. Combine all ingredients in a small bowl, stirring with a whisk. **Yield:** 4 servings (serving size: 1½ tablespoons).

Per serving: CALORIES 52; FAT 3.6g (sat 0.3g, mono 2.1g, poly 1g); PROTEIN 0.1g; CARB 5.8g; FIBER 0.2g; CHOL 0mg; IRON 0.1mg; SODIUM 236mg; CALC 5mg

Menu

PointsPlus value
per serving: 7

BLT Steak Salad

1 (1-ounce) slice toasted
ciabatta bread
PointsPlus value
per serving: 2

Game Plan

1. While skillet heats:
• Prepare bacon.

2. While steak cooks:
• Toast ciabatta bread.

3. While steak rests:
• Rinse and tear lettuce.
• Halve tomatoes.

4. Assemble salad.

BLT Steak Salad

prep: 7 minutes • **cook:** 9 minutes • **other:** 5 minutes
PointsPlus value per serving: 5

All of the high-flavor ingredients of a BLT sandwich are combined with beef tenderloin in this hearty, restaurant-quality salad. If 4-ounce steaks are hard to find, buy an 8-ounce steak from the meat case and cut it in half crosswise.

     4 precooked bacon slices
     2 (4-ounce) beef tenderloin steaks (about 1¼ inches thick), trimmed
     ½ teaspoon salt
     ½ teaspoon freshly ground black pepper
   Cooking spray
     6 cups torn romaine lettuce
     1 cup grape tomatoes, halved
     ½ cup light blue cheese dressing (such as Marie's)

1. Heat bacon according to package directions; crumble and set aside.
2. Sprinkle steaks evenly with salt and pepper; coat both sides with cooking spray.
3. Heat a medium nonstick skillet over medium-high heat. Add steaks; cook 4 to 5 minutes on each side or until desired degree of doneness. Remove steaks from pan; let stand 5 minutes. Cut each steak diagonally across grain into thin slices.
4. Combine lettuce, tomato, and sliced steak in a large bowl; toss well. Divide salad evenly among 4 plates; drizzle dressing evenly over salads. Sprinkle with crumbled bacon. **Yield:** 4 servings (serving size: 2 cups salad, 1½ ounces steak, 2 tablespoons dressing, and 1 tablespoon crumbled bacon).

Per serving: CALORIES 219; FAT 9.7g (sat 2.9g, mono 4g, poly 1.1g); PROTEIN 20.3g; CARB 11.1g; FIBER 2.6g; CHOL 54mg; IRON 1.9mg; SODIUM 786mg; CALC 42mg

Spinach Salad with Grilled Pork Tenderloin and Nectarines

prep: 6 minutes • **cook:** 10 minutes • **other:** 10 minutes
PointsPlus value per serving: 4

Grilling heightens the sweetness and flavor of the nectarines. Because they have such thin skins, nectarines don't require peeling for this dish. However, you may substitute fresh peeled peaches if you prefer.

1   (1-pound) peppercorn-flavored pork tenderloin, trimmed
3   nectarines, halved
Cooking spray
2   (6-ounce) packages fresh baby spinach
¼   cup light balsamic vinaigrette
¼   cup (1 ounce) crumbled feta cheese
Freshly ground black pepper (optional)

1. Prepare grill.

2. Cut pork horizontally through center of meat, cutting to, but not through, other side using a sharp knife; open flat as you would a book. Place pork and nectarine halves, cut sides down, on grill rack coated with cooking spray. Grill pork 5 minutes on each side or until a thermometer registers 160°. Grill nectarine halves 4 to 5 minutes on each side or until thoroughly heated. Remove pork and nectarine halves from grill. Let pork rest 10 minutes.

3. Cut nectarine halves into slices. Thinly slice pork. Combine spinach and vinaigrette in a large bowl; toss gently to coat.

4. Divide spinach mixture evenly among 6 plates. Top each serving evenly with nectarine slices and pork slices. Sprinkle with cheese. Sprinkle evenly with pepper, if desired. **Yield:** 6 servings (serving size: 1⅔ cups spinach salad, ½ nectarine, about 2 ounces pork, and 2 teaspoons cheese).

Per serving: CALORIES 169; FAT 6g (sat 2g, mono 1.5g, poly 0.9g); PROTEIN 16g; CARB 15.8g; FIBER 3.9g; CHOL 41mg; IRON 2.9mg; SODIUM 766mg; CALC 86mg

Menu
PointsPlus value
per serving: 5

Spinach Salad with Grilled Pork
Tenderloin and Nectarines

2 sesame flatbread crackers
PointsPlus value
per serving: 1

Game Plan

1. While grill heats:
   • Cut pork.
   • Rinse and halve
     nectarines.

2. Grill pork and nectarines.

3. While pork rests:
   • Slice nectarines.
   • Divide spinach.

4. Assemble salad.

pictured on page 115

Grilled Romaine Chicken Caesar Salad

prep: 11 minutes • **cook:** 14 minutes   *PointsPlus* value per serving: 8

Grilling sturdy hearts of romaine imparts smoky flavor to this popular salad green. You'll love the contrasting textures of the lightly wilted outer leaves and the crisp center.

Menu
PointsPlus value
per serving: 8

**Grilled Romaine Chicken
Caesar Salad**

Game Plan

1. While grill heats:
  • Halve romaine hearts.
  • Season chicken.
  • Slice French bread.

2. While chicken, romaine,
and bread grill:
  • Prepare dressing.

3. Assemble salad.

 3 (6-ounce) skinless, boneless chicken breast halves
 2 teaspoons olive oil
 ¾ teaspoon freshly ground black pepper, divided
 ½ teaspoon salt, divided
 2 romaine hearts, cut in half lengthwise
    Olive oil–flavored cooking spray
 4 (1-ounce) slices French bread baguette (1 inch thick)
    Caesar Dressing

1. Prepare grill.

2. Brush chicken with olive oil; sprinkle with ½ teaspoon pepper and ¼ teaspoon salt. Coat romaine hearts with cooking spray, and sprinkle with remaining ¼ teaspoon pepper and salt. Coat both sides of bread slices generously with cooking spray.

3. Place chicken, romaine, and bread on grill rack coated with cooking spray. Grill chicken 7 to 8 minutes on each side or until done. Grill romaine halves 4 to 5 minutes. Grill bread slices 3 minutes on each side or until toasted.

4. Cut chicken diagonally into thin slices; cut grilled bread into large cubes. Arrange chicken strips and grilled croutons evenly over romaine halves; drizzle evenly with Caesar Dressing. **Yield:** 4 servings (serving size: 1 romaine heart half, about 4 ounces chicken, ¼ cup croutons, and 3 tablespoons dressing).

Per serving: CALORIES 320; FAT 9.1g (sat 3.6g, mono 3g, poly 2.2g); PROTEIN 37.6g; CARB 21.1g; FIBER 1.8g; CHOL 84mg; IRON 2.9mg; SODIUM 731mg; CALC 203mg

Caesar Dressing

prep: 4 minutes   *PointsPlus* value per serving: 2

 ½ cup nonfat buttermilk
 ¼ cup (1 ounce) shredded fresh Parmigiano-Reggiano cheese
 2 tablespoons light mayonnaise
 ½ teaspoon freshly ground black pepper
 ½ teaspoon Dijon mustard
 2 garlic cloves, pressed

1. Combine all ingredients, stirring with a whisk until smooth. **Yield:** ¾ cup (serving size: 3 tablespoons).

Per serving: CALORIES 69; FAT 4.7g (sat 1.9g, mono 1g, poly 1.4g); PROTEIN 4.3g; CARB 3.1g; FIBER 0.1g; CHOL 10mg; IRON 0.1mg; SODIUM 188mg; CALC 102mg

Chicken, Spinach, and Blueberry Salad with Pomegranate Vinaigrette

prep: 6 minutes • **cook:** 7 minutes   *PointsPlus* value per serving: 5

Sweet blueberries pair well with distinctive blue cheese in this chicken salad, while a bold-flavored vinaigrette lightly coats the tender baby spinach leaves.

Cooking spray
8   chicken breast tenders (about ¾ pound)
1½ teaspoons coarsely ground black pepper
¼   teaspoon salt
8   cups bagged baby spinach
Pomegranate Vinaigrette
½   cup thinly sliced red onion
1   cup fresh blueberries
¼   cup (1 ounce) crumbled blue cheese

1. Heat a grill pan or large nonstick skillet over medium-high heat. Coat pan with cooking spray. Sprinkle chicken with pepper and salt. Coat chicken with cooking spray, and add to pan. Cook 3 to 4 minutes on each side or until done.

2. Divide spinach evenly among 4 plates; drizzle evenly with Pomegranate Vinaigrette. Arrange chicken, onion, and blueberries evenly over spinach. Sprinkle evenly with cheese. **Yield:** 4 servings (serving size: 2 cups spinach, 2 chicken tenders, 3 tablespoons vinaigrette, 2 tablespoons onion, ¼ cup blueberries, and 1 tablespoon cheese).

Per serving: CALORIES 203; FAT 4.4g (sat 1.7g, mono 1.6g, poly 0.7g); PROTEIN 23g; CARB 18.5g; FIBER 3.7g; CHOL 56mg; IRON 2.4mg; SODIUM 377mg; CALC 95mg

Pomegranate Vinaigrette

prep: 2 minutes   *PointsPlus* value per serving: 3

½   cup pomegranate juice
3   tablespoons sugar
3   tablespoons balsamic vinegar
1   tablespoon canola oil
1   teaspoon grated orange rind

1. Combine all ingredients in a small bowl. Stir with a whisk until blended. **Yield:** ¾ cup (serving size: 3 tablespoons).

Per serving: CALORIES 96; FAT 3.5g (sat 0.3g, mono 2.1g, poly 1g); PROTEIN 0.2g; CARB 15.9g; FIBER 0.1g; CHOL 0mg; IRON 0.1mg; SODIUM 7mg; CALC 9mg

---

Menu
PointsPlus value per serving: 5

Chicken, Spinach, and Blueberry Salad with Pomegranate Vinaigrette

Game Plan

1. While grill pan heats:
   • Season chicken.
   • Slice onion.

2. While chicken cooks:
   • Prepare dressing.
   • Divide spinach on plates.

3. Assemble salad.

pictured on page 116

Menu
PointsPlus value
per serving: 6

Chicken Salad with Red Grapes
and Citrus-Honey Dressing

Game Plan

1. Prepare dressing.

2. Assemble salad.

Chicken Salad with Red Grapes and Citrus-Honey Dressing

prep: 10 minutes   *PointsPlus* value per serving: 6

In this unique sweet-savory tossed salad, juicy red grapes offer a surprising contrast to the tangy citrus dressing. You'll need to squeeze about 2 medium lemons to yield ¼ cup lemon juice for the dressing.

  8   cups mixed baby salad greens
  2   cups shredded cooked chicken breast (about 8 ounces)
  1   cup seedless red grapes, halved
  ⅔   cup thin diagonally cut slices celery
Citrus-Honey Dressing

1. Combine all ingredients in a large bowl; toss gently. Place 2 cups salad on each of 4 plates. **Yield:** 4 servings (serving size: 1 salad).

Per serving: CALORIES 230; FAT 9.4g (sat 1.6g, mono 6.1g, poly 1.2g); PROTEIN 19.9g; CARB 17.8g; FIBER 3.2g; CHOL 48mg; IRON 2.3mg; SODIUM 323mg; CALC 85mg

Citrus-Honey Dressing

prep: 5 minutes   *PointsPlus* value per serving: 3

  ¼   cup fresh lemon juice
  2   tablespoons fresh orange juice
  2   tablespoons extra-virgin olive oil
  1   tablespoon honey
  2   teaspoons grated lemon rind
  ½   teaspoon kosher salt
  ⅛   teaspoon coarsely ground black pepper

1. Combine all ingredients in a small bowl, stirring with a whisk. **Yield:** ½ cup (serving size: 2 tablespoons).

Per serving: CALORIES 87; FAT 7g (sat 1g, mono 5.4g, poly 0.6g); PROTEIN 0.2g; CARB 6.7g; FIBER 0.2g; CHOL 0mg; IRON 0.1mg; SODIUM 236mg; CALC 4mg

Grilled Chicken and Vegetable Arugula Salad

prep: 4 minutes • **cook:** 6 minutes   *PointsPlus* value per serving: 6

This colorful salad is packed with garden-fresh zucchini and tomatoes. Grill the bread slices along with the tomatoes so everything is ready at the same time.

    4   (4-ounce) chicken cutlets
    7   tablespoons light balsamic vinaigrette (such as Newman's Own), divided
    1   medium zucchini (8 ounces), cut in half lengthwise
    6   (¼-inch-thick) slices red onion (1 medium)
    Cooking spray
    4   plum tomatoes, halved
    6   cups baby arugula
    ½   cup (2 ounces) crumbled feta cheese

1. Prepare grill.

2. Brush chicken with 1 tablespoon vinaigrette. Place chicken, zucchini, and onion on grill rack coated with cooking spray. Grill 3 to 4 minutes on each side or until chicken is done and vegetables are tender, adding tomato halves to grill rack after 2 minutes. Cook tomato 2 minutes on each side. Remove chicken and vegetables from grill. Cut chicken crosswise into thin slices; coarsely chop vegetables.

3. Combine chicken, vegetables, and remaining 6 tablespoons vinaigrette in a large bowl, tossing to coat. Add arugula and cheese; toss gently. **Yield:** 4 servings (serving size: 2¾ cups).

Per serving: CALORIES 243; FAT 8.4g (sat 3g, mono 2g, poly 2.6g); PROTEIN 30.6g; CARB 11.1g; FIBER 2.5g; CHOL 78mg; IRON 1.8mg; SODIUM 661mg; CALC 153mg

Menu
PointsPlus value per serving: 8

Grilled Chicken and Vegetable Arugula Salad

Grilled Garlic Bread

Game Plan

1. While grill heats:
   • Cut zucchini.
   • Slice onion.
   • Halve tomatoes.

2. While chicken and vegetables grill:
   • Prepare and grill garlic bread.

3. Chop and assemble salad.

Grilled Garlic Bread

prep: 2 minutes • **cook:** 4 minutes   *PointsPlus* value per serving: 2

    4   (0.07-ounce) Italian bread slices
    1   garlic clove, halved
    2   teaspoons extra-virgin olive oil
    Cooking spray

1. Prepare grill.

2. Rub bread slices with cut sides of garlic halves; brush evenly with oil. Place bread slices on grill rack coated with cooking spray. Grill 2 minutes on each side or until lightly toasted. **Yield:** 4 servings (serving size: 1 slice).

Per serving: CALORIES 75; FAT 3g (sat 0.5g, mono 1.8g, poly 0.6g); PROTEIN 1.8g; CARB 10.2g; FIBER 0.6g; CHOL 0mg; IRON 0.6mg; SODIUM 116mg; CALC 17mg

Menu
PointsPlus value
per serving: 4

Chicken Salad with Asparagus and Creamy Dill Dressing

1 cup cubed melon
PointsPlus value
per serving: 0

Game Plan

1. While asparagus steams:
  • Slice tomatoes and radishes.
  • Prepare dressing.

2. Assemble salad.

Chicken Salad with Asparagus and Creamy Dill Dressing

prep: 3 minutes • **cook:** 5 minutes   *PointsPlus* value per serving: 4

This tasty salad is perfect for evenings when you're looking for a quick, no-fuss meal. We hand-pulled large pieces of chicken from a cooked chicken breast to achieve a chunky texture. Serve with crackers to complete the meal.

2½   cups (2-inch) diagonally cut asparagus
2   cups coarsely shredded cooked chicken breast (about 8 ounces)
½   cup thinly sliced radishes
Creamy Dill Dressing
8   tomato slices (about 1 large)
Freshly ground black pepper (optional)

1. Steam asparagus, covered, 3 minutes or until crisp-tender. Drain and plunge asparagus into ice water; drain.
2. Combine asparagus, chicken, radishes, and dressing in a large bowl; toss well. Arrange 2 tomato slices on each of 4 plates; top each serving with 1 cup chicken mixture. Sprinkle with pepper, if desired. **Yield:** 4 servings (serving size: 1 salad).

Per serving: CALORIES 170; FAT 4.3g (sat 0.6g, mono 1.7g, poly 1.5g); PROTEIN 21.2g; CARB 12.2g; FIBER 2.8g; CHOL 49mg; IRON 2.6mg; SODIUM 467mg; CALC 79mg

Creamy Dill Dressing

prep: 4 minutes   *PointsPlus* value per serving: 1

½   cup light mayonnaise
½   cup nonfat buttermilk
1   tablespoon chopped fresh dill
1   tablespoon fresh lemon juice
¼   teaspoon kosher salt
¼   teaspoon freshly ground black pepper

1. Combine all ingredients in a medium bowl, stirring well with a whisk. **Yield:** 8 servings (serving size: 2 tablespoons).

Per serving: CALORIES 21; FAT 1g (sat 0g, mono 0g, poly 0.5g); PROTEIN 0.6g; CARB 3.1g; FIBER 0g; CHOL 0mg; IRON 0mg; SODIUM 205mg; CALC 19mg

Green Salsa Chicken | page 88

Grilled Sun-Dried Tomato Chicken
Breast | page 82

Grilled Romaine Chicken
Caesar Salad | page 108

Chicken Salad with Red Grapes and Citrus-Honey Dressing | page 110

Grilled Southwestern Shrimp Salad with
Lime-Cumin Dressing | page 105

Grilled Grouper Sandwiches with
Tartar Sauce | page 131

Turkey Antipasto Panini | page 140

Sloppy Skillet Beef Sandwiches | page 134

Spicy Poblano and Corn Soup | page 145

Sausage and Barley Soup | page 152

Banana Pudding Ice Cream Smash | page 185

Fresh Berries with Limoncello-Mint Cream | page 179

Mini Turtle Trifles | page 174

Pineapple-Macadamia Sundaes | page 187

Sandwiches

Menu
PointsPlus value
per serving: 7

Overstuffed Grilled Vegetable-
Feta Sandwich

1 orange
PointsPlus value
per serving: 0

Game Plan

1. While grill heats:
   • Slice onion.
   • Rinse and cut tomatoes and basil.

2. Grill vegetables, and toss with dressing.

3. Grill bread, and assemble sandwiches.

Overstuffed Grilled Vegetable–Feta Sandwiches

prep: 4 minutes • **cook:** 11 minutes   *PointsPlus* value per serving: 7

Make sure your grill is nice and hot to create grill marks on the vegetables and bread.

1⅓ cups refrigerated presliced yellow squash and zucchini mix
4 (¼-inch-thick) slices red onion
Cooking spray
¾ cup grape tomatoes, halved
3 tablespoons light Northern Italian salad dressing with basil and Romano (such as Ken's Steak House Lite)
1 tablespoon chopped fresh basil
1 (8-ounce) loaf French bread, halved lengthwise
¾ cup (3 ounces) crumbled feta cheese

1. Prepare grill.
2. Coat squash mix and onion evenly with cooking spray. Place vegetables on grill rack; grill 4 minutes on each side or until crisp-tender and beginning to brown.
3. Place tomato in a medium bowl; add dressing and basil, tossing gently to coat. Add cooked vegetables to tomato mixture; toss well.
4. Coat cut sides of bread with cooking spray. Grill bread 1 minute on each side or until lightly toasted. Spoon vegetable mixture over bottom half of bread; sprinkle evenly with cheese. Top with remaining bread half. Press down lightly; cut crosswise into 4 equal pieces. **Yield:** 4 servings (serving size: 1 piece).

Per serving: CALORIES 283; FAT 8g (sat 3.5g, mono 1.2g, poly 0.7g); PROTEIN 11.6g; CARB 42.5g; FIBER 3.2g; CHOL 19mg; IRON 2.7mg; SODIUM 773mg; CALC 158mg

pictured on page 118

Grilled Grouper Sandwiches with Tartar Sauce

prep: 6 minutes • **cook:** 6 minutes   *PointsPlus* value per serving: 10

Grouper is a white-meat fish that is well suited for the grill. If you can't find grouper, use sea bass or mahimahi. Look for fish that is free of blemishes, has a fresh smell, and has flesh that springs back when touched.

4   (6-ounce) grouper fillets (about 1½ inches thick)
2   teaspoons olive oil
¼   teaspoon salt
¼   teaspoon black pepper
Cooking spray
Tartar Sauce
4   (1.8-ounce) white-wheat hamburger buns
4   green leaf lettuce leaves

1. Prepare grill.
2. Brush fillets evenly with olive oil; sprinkle evenly with salt and pepper. Place fillets on grill rack coated with cooking spray; grill 3 to 4 minutes on each side or until desired degree of doneness.
3. While fish cooks, prepare Tartar Sauce. Spread about 2½ tablespoons Tartar Sauce over cut side of each bun; place 1 lettuce leaf on bottom half of each bun. Top lettuce with fish; top with remaining bun halves. **Yield:** 4 servings (serving size: 1 sandwich).

Per serving: CALORIES 388; FAT 16g (sat 2.8g, mono 2g, poly 1.9g); PROTEIN 38.5g; CARB 26.3g; FIBER 5.5g; CHOL 73mg; IRON 4.6mg; SODIUM 783mg; CALC 311mg

Tartar Sauce

prep: 4 minutes   *PointsPlus* value per serving: 1

½   cup light mayonnaise
2   tablespoons chopped green onions
1   tablespoon sweet pickle relish
1½   teaspoons capers, drained
1½   teaspoons fresh lemon juice
½   teaspoon Worcestershire sauce

1. Combine all ingredients in a small bowl, stirring with a whisk until well blended. **Yield:** ⅔ cup (serving size: about 1 tablespoon).

Per serving: CALORIES 43; FAT 4g (sat 0.6g, mono 0g, poly 0g); PROTEIN 0.1g; CARB 1.8g; FIBER 0.1g; CHOL 4mg; IRON 0.1mg; SODIUM 124mg; CALC 2mg

---

Menu
PointsPlus value
per serving: 10

Grilled Grouper Sandwich with Tartar Sauce

Game Plan

1. While grill heats:
• Season fish.

2. While fish grills:
• Prepare tartar sauce.

3. Assemble sandwich.

Tilapia Sandwiches with Greek Tapenade

prep: 8 minutes • **cook:** 6 minutes   *PointsPlus* value per serving: 9

Mâche, also known as lamb's lettuce or corn salad, is a tender green with a tangy, nutty flavor. Look for it in the produce section at your supermarket. Use a mini food processor—or take your time using a large chef's knife—to finely chop the olives, roasted bell peppers, and oregano for the Greek Tapenade before you spread the mixture over the toasted bread.

Greek Tapenade
2 (6-ounce) tilapia fillets
⅛ teaspoon salt
⅛ teaspoon coarsely ground black pepper
Cooking spray
4 (0.8-ounce) slices crusty Chicago-style Italian bread (about ½ inch thick), toasted
4 tomato slices
⅔ cup mâche

1. Prepare Greek Tapenade; set aside.

2. Sprinkle fillets evenly with salt and pepper. Heat a large nonstick skillet over medium-high heat; coat pan with cooking spray. Add fish; cook 2 to 3 minutes on each side or until desired degree of doneness.

3. Spread about 1 tablespoon Greek Tapenade on each bread slice. Top each of 2 bread slices with 1 fillet, 2 tomato slices, ⅓ cup mâche, and remaining bread slices.
Yield: 2 servings (serving size: 1 sandwich).

Per serving: CALORIES 347; FAT 8.9g (sat 3g, mono 3.4g, poly 1.7g); PROTEIN 39.9g; CARB 26g; FIBER 1.6g; CHOL 93mg; IRON 3mg; SODIUM 768mg; CALC 113mg

Greek Tapenade

prep: 5 minutes   *PointsPlus* value per serving: 1

2 tablespoons chopped pitted kalamata olives
2 tablespoons crumbled feta cheese
1 tablespoon chopped bottled roasted red bell peppers
½ teaspoon grated lemon rind
1 teaspoon fresh lemon juice
½ teaspoon chopped fresh oregano

1. Place all ingredients in a mini food processor; pulse 2 or 3 times or until minced.
Yield: 2 servings (serving size: 2½ tablespoons).

Per serving: CALORIES 52; FAT 4.3g (sat 1.7g, mono 2.2g, poly 0.3g); PROTEIN 1.5g; CARB 1.7g; FIBER 0.1g; CHOL 8mg; IRON 0mg; SODIUM 262mg; CALC 52mg

Tuna Florentine Sandwiches with Lemon-Caper Vinaigrette

prep: 4 minutes • **cook:** 3 minutes   *PointsPlus* value per serving: 8

Fresh basil leaves and a homemade lemon-caper vinaigrette lend a vibrant Italian flair to this easy sandwich.

1	(12-ounce) can albacore tuna in water, drained and flaked
1½	cups bagged baby spinach leaves
1	cup fresh basil leaves
	Lemon-Caper Vinaigrette
8	(1.5-ounce) multigrain bread slices (such as Arnold Healthy Multigrain), toasted

1. Combine first 4 ingredients; toss well. Spoon tuna mixture evenly over each of 4 toasted bread slices. Top with remaining bread slices. **Yield:** 4 servings (serving size: 1 sandwich).

Per serving: CALORIES 326; FAT 7.2g (sat 0.5g, mono 2.9g, poly 2.9g); PROTEIN 25.3g; CARB 43.1g; FIBER 6g; CHOL 26mg; IRON 3.3mg; SODIUM 572mg; CALC 291mg

Lemon-Caper Vinaigrette

prep: 4 minutes   *PointsPlus* value per serving: 1

3	tablespoons fresh lemon juice
2½	tablespoons minced shallots (1 small)
1	tablespoon drained capers
1	tablespoon olive oil
½	teaspoon freshly ground black pepper
½	teaspoon Dijon mustard

1. Combine all ingredients in a small bowl, stirring with a whisk. **Yield:** ½ cup (serving size: 2 tablespoons).

Per serving: CALORIES 39; FAT 3.5g (sat 0.5g, mono 2.5g, poly 0.5g); PROTEIN 0.4g; CARB 2.4g; FIBER 0.2g; CHOL 0mg; IRON 0.1mg; SODIUM 63mg; CALC 6mg

---

Menu
PointsPlus value per serving: 8

Tuna Florentine Sandwich with Lemon-Caper Vinaigrette

Game Plan

1. Prepare vinaigrette.

2. While assembling tuna Florentine:
  • Toast bread.

3. Assemble sandwiches.

pictured on page 120

Sloppy Skillet Beef Sandwiches

prep: 2 minutes • **cook:** 15 minutes   *PointsPlus* value per serving: 10

Add color, crunch, and—most importantly—convenience to this weeknight family favorite with prechopped yellow, red, and green bell pepper.

Menu
PointsPlus value per serving: 12

Sloppy Skillet Beef Sandwiches

Sweet and Tangy Mustard Coleslaw

Game Plan

1. While beef and bell peppers sauté:
• Assemble coleslaw.

2. Drain beef and cook.

3. Assemble sandwiches.

Cooking spray
1 pound lean ground beef
1 cup refrigerated prechopped tricolor bell pepper mix
½ cup frozen whole-kernel corn
1 (14.5-ounce) can Mexican-style stewed tomatoes with jalapeño peppers and spices, undrained
¼ cup plus 2 tablespoons ketchup
4 (1½-ounce) whole-wheat hamburger buns

1. Heat a large nonstick skillet over medium-high heat. Coat pan with cooking spray. Add beef and bell pepper; sauté 5 minutes or until meat is browned, stirring to crumble. Drain well; return meat mixture to pan. Add corn, tomatoes, and ketchup; cook 9 minutes or to desired consistency. Serve on hamburger buns. **Yield:** 4 servings (serving size: 1 cup beef and 1 bun).

Per serving: CALORIES 382; FAT 13g (sat 4.5g, mono 5g, poly 1.5g); PROTEIN 29.1g; CARB 41.2g; FIBER 6.1g; CHOL 41mg; IRON 4.1mg; SODIUM 864mg; CALC 79mg

Sweet and Tangy Mustard Coleslaw

prep: 5 minutes   *PointsPlus* value per serving: 2

2 tablespoons sugar
1 tablespoon canola oil
1 tablespoon cider vinegar
1 tablespoon prepared mustard
¼ teaspoon salt
4 cups packaged cabbage-and-carrot coleslaw
½ cup refrigerated prechopped tricolor bell pepper mix

1. Combine first 5 ingredients in a large bowl; stir well with a whisk. Add coleslaw and bell pepper; toss gently to coat. **Yield:** 4 servings (serving size: 1 cup).

Per serving: CALORIES 75; FAT 4g (sat 0.3g, mono 2.2g, poly 1.1g); PROTEIN 0.8g; CARB 9.9g; FIBER 1.4g; CHOL 0mg; IRON 0.3mg; SODIUM 196mg; CALC 24mg

Hamburger Panini Sliders

prep: 6 minutes • **cook:** 12 minutes   *PointsPlus* value per serving: 8

A panini press or tabletop electric grill also works well for pressing and grilling these mini burgers.

1   pound extra-lean ground beef
3   tablespoons commercial pesto
Cooking spray
8   (1.25-ounce) wheat slider buns
4   (0.75-ounce) slices reduced-fat provolone cheese
8   fresh basil leaves

1. Combine beef and pesto. Divide mixture into 8 equal portions, shaping each into a ½-inch-thick patty.

2. Heat a large nonstick skillet over medium-high heat. Coat pan with cooking spray. Place patties in pan; cook 2 minutes on each side or until done.

3. Place 1 patty on bottom half of each bun; top each with ½ slice cheese, 1 basil leaf, and top half of bun.

4. Heat a large grill pan over medium heat. Coat pan with cooking spray. Add burgers to pan. Place a cast-iron or other heavy skillet on top of burgers; press gently to flatten sandwiches. Cook 2 minutes or until cheese melts and bread is toasted.

Yield: 8 servings (serving size: 1 slider).

Per serving: CALORIES 223; FAT 9g (sat 2.8g, mono 3.6g, poly 1.4g); PROTEIN 19.9g; CARB 17.4g; FIBER 1.2g; CHOL 37mg; IRON 2mg; SODIUM 306mg; CALC 166mg

Menu
PointsPlus value
per serving: 8

Hamburger Panini Sliders

1 cup mixed baby greens tossed with fat-free vinaigrette
PointsPlus value
per serving: 0

Game Plan

1. Season and cook beef.

2. Assemble sandwiches.

3. While sandwiches cook:
 • Toss salad.

Menu
PointsPlus value
per serving: 9

**Sweet-Spiked Pork
Sandwiches**

Spicy Celery Seed Coleslaw

Game Plan

1. While pork cooks:
- Toast bread.
- Prepare coleslaw.

2. While pork rests:
- Cook cola and bourbon mixture.

3. Assemble sandwiches.

Sweet-Spiked Pork Sandwiches

prep: 2 minutes • **cook:** 25 minutes • **other:** 5 minutes
PointsPlus value per serving: 7

　1　(1-pound) pork tenderloin, trimmed
　¾　teaspoon coarsely ground black pepper
　¼　teaspoon salt
　　　Cooking spray
　1　cup cola
　¼　cup bourbon
2½　tablespoons country-style Dijon mustard
　4　(0.8-ounce) Chicago Italian bread slices, lightly toasted

1. Sprinkle pork evenly with pepper and salt; coat with cooking spray. Heat a large nonstick skillet over medium-high heat. Coat pan with cooking spray. Add pork; cook 3 minutes or until browned on 1 side.

2. Reduce heat to medium-low; turn pork over. Cover and cook 17 minutes or until a thermometer registers 160° (slightly pink). Remove pork from pan. Cover and let stand 5 minutes.

3. While pork stands, increase heat to medium-high, and add cola and bourbon to pan. Bring to a boil; cook 7 minutes or until mixture is reduced to ¼ cup.

4. Spread mustard evenly on 1 side of bread slices. Cut pork into thin slices. Add pork slices to sauce, tossing to coat. Arrange pork slices over mustard. Spoon sauce evenly over pork. **Yield:** 4 servings (serving size: 1 open-faced sandwich).

Per serving: CALORIES 275; FAT 4.7g (sat 1.5g, mono 1.9g, poly 0.7g); PROTEIN 25.9g; CARB 20.1g; FIBER 0.7g; CHOL 74mg; IRON 2.1mg; SODIUM 562mg; CALC 27mg

Spicy Celery Seed Coleslaw

prep: 5 minutes　　　　　　　　　　　　　*PointsPlus* value per serving: 2

　1　tablespoon sugar
　3　tablespoons light mayonnaise
　1　tablespoon water
　1　teaspoon cider vinegar
　½　teaspoon celery seed
　¼　teaspoon freshly ground black pepper
　⅛　teaspoon crushed red pepper
　⅛　teaspoon salt
　3　cups cabbage-and-carrot coleslaw

1. Combine all ingredients, except coleslaw, in a medium bowl; stir with a whisk. Add coleslaw; toss well. **Yield:** 4 servings (serving size: about ⅔ cup).

Per serving: CALORIES 61; FAT 3.8g (sat 0.8g, mono 1g, poly 2g); PROTEIN 0.4g; CARB 6g; FIBER 0.8g; CHOL 4mg; IRON 0.3mg; SODIUM 169mg; CALC 20mg

Pressed Italian Sandwich with Pesto

prep: 14 minutes • **other:** 2 hours to 24 hours   *PointsPlus* value per serving: 8

This pressed sandwich can be made a day ahead and stored in the refrigerator until ready to serve—just be sure to layer the red bell pepper strips between the prosciutto and cheese to prevent the bread from becoming soggy.

Menu
PointsPlus value
per serving: 8

**Pressed Italian Sandwich
with Pesto**

Game Plan

1. Prepare pesto.

2. Assemble sandwich, and refrigerate.

1   (16-ounce) ciabatta bread
Pesto
6   ounces very thinly sliced prosciutto
1   cup bottled roasted red bell pepper, cut into strips
8   (0.75-ounce) slices mozzarella cheese
¼   teaspoon freshly ground black pepper

1. Slice ciabatta in half horizontally. Hollow out top and bottom halves of bread; reserve torn bread for another use. Spread Pesto over bottom half of bread. Layer prosciutto, bell pepper strips, and cheese over pesto; sprinkle with black pepper. Replace top half of bread. Wrap loaf in plastic wrap and foil, and place on a plate; top with a heavy skillet filled with heavy cans. Refrigerate 2 hours or overnight.
2. Remove foil and plastic wrap; cut sandwich into 8 pieces. **Yield:** 8 servings (serving size: 1 piece).

Per serving: CALORIES 313; FAT 13g (sat 4.6g, mono 6.1g, poly 1.4g); PROTEIN 17.2g; CARB 33.2g; FIBER 1.5g; CHOL 27mg; IRON 2.5mg; SODIUM 987mg; CALC 224mg

Pesto

prep: 9 minutes   *PointsPlus* value per serving: 1

1   tablespoon pine nuts
1   garlic clove
2   cups fresh basil leaves
¼   cup (1 ounce) grated fresh Parmesan cheese
1½ tablespoons olive oil
⅛   teaspoon salt

1. With food processor on, drop pine nuts and garlic through food chute; process until minced. Add basil and remaining ingredients; process until smooth. **Yield:** about ½ cup (serving size: about 1 tablespoon).

Per serving: CALORIES 48; FAT 4.3g (sat 0.9g, mono 2.1g, poly 0.7g); PROTEIN 1.9g; CARB 0.7g; FIBER 0.4g; CHOL 3mg; IRON 0.4mg; SODIUM 100mg; CALC 67mg

Menu

PointsPlus value
per serving: 9

Sun-Dried Tomato Turkey
Burgers with Basil Aioli

Game Plan

1. While grill heats:
  • Combine turkey mixture, and shape into patties.

2. While burgers grill:
  • Prepare aioli.

3. Assemble burgers.

Sun-Dried Tomato Turkey Burgers with Basil Aioli

prep: 5 minutes • **cook:** 6 minutes   *PointsPlus* value per serving: 9

Take turkey burgers to a new level with three big-flavor ingredients—goat cheese, sun-dried tomatoes, and Basil Aioli.

1¼   pounds ground turkey breast
¼   cup (2 ounces) crumbled goat cheese
¼   cup chopped drained oil-packed sun-dried tomato halves
¼   teaspoon salt
⅛   teaspoon black pepper
Cooking spray
  4   green leaf lettuce leaves (optional)
  4   (1.8-ounce) white-wheat hamburger buns (such as Nature's Own)
  4   tomato slices (optional)
Basil Aioli

1. Prepare grill.

2. Combine first 5 ingredients. Divide turkey mixture into 4 equal portions, shaping each into a ½-inch patty.

3. Place patties on grill rack coated with cooking spray; grill 8 minutes on each side or until a thermometer registers 165°.

4. Place 1 lettuce leaf, if desired, on bottom half of each bun; top each with 1 burger and, if desired, 1 tomato slice. Spread 1 tablespoon Basil Aioli on inside of each bun top. Place tops on burgers. **Yield:** 4 servings (serving size: 1 burger).

Per serving: CALORIES 356; FAT 12.8g (sat 4.1g, mono 4.3g, poly 3.2g); PROTEIN 41g; CARB 24.3g; FIBER 5.5g; CHOL 69mg; IRON 1.4mg; SODIUM 805mg; CALC 326mg

Basil Aioli

prep: 3 minutes   *PointsPlus* value per serving: 1

¼   cup light mayonnaise
  2   teaspoons chopped fresh basil
¼   teaspoon salt
  1   garlic clove, minced

1. Combine all ingredients in a small bowl, stirring with a whisk. **Yield:** ¼ cup (serving size: 1 tablespoon).

Per serving: CALORIES 51; FAT 4.9g (sat 0.8g, mono 1.2g, poly 2.7g); PROTEIN 0.2g; CARB 1.5g; FIBER 0.1g; CHOL 5mg; IRON 0.1mg; SODIUM 265mg; CALC 3mg

Turkey Cobb Sandwiches

prep: 10 minutes *PointsPlus* value per serving: 8

Bookend the traditional ingredients of a Cobb salad with two slices of fresh wheat bread, and you've got a flavorful Turkey Cobb Sandwich. As an added convenience, you can now purchase boiled eggs at your supermarket. If you can't find them in your local store, hardcook your own a day ahead. It will make preparation for this recipe quick and easy. Serve the sandwich with waffle-cut carrot chips and celery sticks.

2	tablespoons reduced-fat mayonnaise
8	(1-ounce) slices double-fiber wheat bread (such as Nature's Own), toasted
4	small green leaf lettuce leaves
4	tomato slices
6	ounces shaved deli turkey
1	peeled avocado, sliced
4	precooked bacon slices
2	hard-cooked large eggs, sliced

1. Spread ½ tablespoon mayonnaise evenly over each of 4 bread slices. Layer each evenly with lettuce and next 5 ingredients. Top with remaining 4 bread slices. Cut each sandwich in half diagonally. **Yield:** 4 servings (serving size: 1 sandwich).

Per serving: CALORIES 319; FAT 14.9g (sat 2.7g, mono 5.9g, poly 1.9g); PROTEIN 22.1g; CARB 32.1g; FIBER 12.9g; CHOL 126mg; IRON 3.5mg; SODIUM 712mg; CALC 25mg

Menu
PointsPlus value
per serving: 8

Turkey Cobb Sandwich

1 cup carrot chips and celery sticks
PointsPlus value
per serving: 0

Game Plan

1. While bread toasts:
• Slice tomato, avocado, and egg.

2. Assemble sandwiches.

pictured on page 119

Turkey Antipasto Panini

prep: 7 minutes • **cook:** 3 minutes   *PointsPlus* value per serving: 9

 2 tablespoons reduced-fat mayonnaise
 8 (0.9-ounce) slices crusty Chicago-style Italian bread
 8 ounces shaved lower-sodium deli turkey (such as Boar's Head)
 1 (6-ounce) jar quartered marinated artichoke hearts, drained and coarsely chopped
 ½ cup moist sun-dried tomato halves, packed without oil and sliced
 ½ cup sliced bottled roasted red bell peppers
 12 basil leaves
 4 (1-ounce) slices reduced-fat provolone cheese (such as Alpine Lace)
 Cooking spray

1. Preheat panini grill.
2. Spread mayonnaise evenly over bread slices. Top each of 4 bread slices evenly with turkey, artichokes, tomato, bell pepper, basil leaves, and cheese. Top with remaining bread slices. Coat both sides of sandwiches with cooking spray.
3. Place sandwiches on panini grill. Grill 3 to 4 minutes or until bread is browned and cheese melts. Cut panini in half before serving, if desired. **Yield:** 4 servings (serving size: 1 sandwich).

Per serving: CALORIES 361; FAT 10g (sat 3.5g, mono 0.4g, poly 1.2g); PROTEIN 26.9g; CARB 39.8g; FIBER 4.5g; CHOL 35mg; IRON 3.1mg; SODIUM 1087mg; CALC 83mg

Italian Berry Float

prep: 5 minutes   *PointsPlus* value per serving: 7

 2 cups blood orange or lemon sorbet
 2 cups mixed berries (such as raspberries, strawberries, blackberries, and blueberries)
 2 cups Prosecco or other sparkling wine
 Mint sprigs

1. Place ½ cup sorbet in each of 4 glasses. Arrange ½ cup berries evenly around sorbet in each glass. Pour ½ cup Prosecco over berries in each glass; garnish with mint sprigs. Serve immediately. **Yield:** 4 servings (serving size: 1 float).

Per serving: CALORIES 203; FAT 0.3g (sat 0g, mono 0g, poly 0.2g); PROTEIN 0.6g; CARB 30.4g; FIBER 2.7g; CHOL 0mg; IRON 0.4mg; SODIUM 34mg; CALC 13mg

Soups

Menu
PointsPlus value
per serving: 9

Jamaican Red Beans and
Rice Soup

Game Plan

1. While onion and bacon
cook:
 • Heat broth.
 • Rinse and drain beans.

2. Boil broth-bacon mixture.

3. Add rice and simmer.

Jamaican Red Beans and Rice Soup

prep: 3 minutes • **cook:** 11 minutes   *PointsPlus* value per serving: 9

This quick recipe is loaded with beans and rice, making this soup a filling one-dish meal. Mashing the beans slightly adds body.

½   cup chopped onion (1 small)
2   bacon slices, cut crosswise into thin strips
2   (14-ounce) cans fat-free, lower-sodium chicken broth
2   teaspoons Jamaican jerk seasoning (such as McCormick)
1   (16-ounce) can red beans, rinsed and drained (such as Bush's)
1   (8.8-ounce) package microwaveable precooked whole-grain brown rice (such as Uncle Ben's Ready Rice)
¼   cup chopped fresh cilantro

1. Cook onion and bacon in a large saucepan over medium heat 2 minutes.
2. While bacon mixture cooks, place broth in a large microwave-safe bowl. Cover with plastic wrap; vent. Microwave at HIGH 2 minutes.
3. Add hot broth and jerk seasoning to bacon mixture. Stir in beans, mashing slightly. Cover; bring to a boil over high heat. Uncover, reduce heat, and simmer 5 minutes. Stir in rice; cover and simmer 3 minutes. Ladle soup evenly into 4 bowls; sprinkle with cilantro. **Yield:** 4 servings (serving size: 1¼ cups).

Per serving: CALORIES 375; FAT 7.2g (sat 1.7g, mono 2.6g, poly 0.9g); PROTEIN 11.7g; CARB 65.5g; FIBER 7.7g; CHOL 8mg; IRON 2.1mg; SODIUM 887mg; CALC 34mg

French Onion Soup

prep: 5 minutes • **cook:** 25 minutes   *PointsPlus* value per serving: 3

Traditionally, cheese toast tops a classic bistro-style French onion soup. However, we decided to omit it from this rich soup and add a gourmet grilled sandwich on the side instead. It's the perfect accompaniment.

 1 tablespoon vegetable oil
 3 sweet onions, cut in half vertically and thinly sliced (about 1¾ pounds)
 5 thyme sprigs
 2 (14-ounce) cans fat-free, lower-sodium beef broth

1. Heat oil in a large Dutch oven over medium-high heat. Add onion and thyme; cover and cook 20 minutes, stirring occasionally. Stir in broth; simmer 4 minutes. Remove and discard thyme. **Yield:** 4 servings (serving size: 1¼ cups).

Per serving: CALORIES 103; FAT 3.7g (sat 0.5g, mono 1.2g, poly 1.7g); PROTEIN 3.4g; CARB 15g; FIBER 1.8g; CHOL 0mg; IRON 0.6mg; SODIUM 415mg; CALC 41mg

Menu
PointsPlus value per serving: 8

French Onion Soup

Gruyère-Thyme Grilled Cheese Sandwich

Game Plan

1. While onion and thyme cook:
  • Combine sandwich spread.

2. Add beef broth to pot and simmer.

3. Assemble and cook sandwiches.

Gruyère-Thyme Grilled Cheese Sandwiches

prep: 4 minutes • **cook:** 6 minutes   *PointsPlus* value per serving: 5

 ¾ cup (3 ounces) Gruyère cheese
 1 teaspoon fresh thyme leaves
 2 teaspoons Dijon mustard
 ¼ teaspoon black pepper
 8 (¼-inch-thick) slices Italian bread (about 5 ounces)
Butter-flavored cooking spray

1. Combine first 4 ingredients in a bowl. Spread filling on 4 bread slices; top with remaining bread slices.
2. Heat a large nonstick skillet over medium-high heat. Coat tops of sandwiches with cooking spray. Arrange sandwiches, top sides down, in pan. Coat sandwiches with cooking spray. Cook 2 to 3 minutes on each side or until cheese melts and bread is golden brown. **Yield:** 4 servings (serving size: 1 sandwich).

Per serving: CALORIES 185; FAT 8.1g (sat 4.3g, mono 2.4g, poly 0.9g); PROTEIN 9.5g; CARB 17.9g; FIBER 1g; CHOL 23mg; IRON 1.1mg; SODIUM 311mg; CALC 244mg

Menu
PointsPlus value
per serving: 11

Pan-Roasted Mushroom and
Wild Rice Soup

Mixed Greens and Raspberries
with Hazelnuts and Raspberry
Vinaigrette

Game Plan

1. While mushrooms and
celery mixture cook:
• Prepare rice.
• Cut cheese.
• Toast hazelnuts.

2. Combine remaining ingredients for soup.

3. While soup thickens:
• Prepare salad.

4. Add rice to soup.

Pan-Roasted Mushroom and Wild Rice Soup

prep: 1 minute • **cook:** 12 minutes   *PointsPlus* value per serving: 6

1   tablespoon olive oil
1   (4-ounce) package gourmet-blend mushrooms
1   cup refrigerated prechopped celery, onion, and bell pepper mix
1   (2.75-ounce) package quick-cooking wild rice (such as Gourmet House)
1   (6-ounce) package light garlic-and-herb spreadable cheese wedges (such as The Laughing Cow)
2   cups 1% low-fat milk
½   teaspoon dried thyme
½   teaspoon freshly ground black pepper
¼   teaspoon salt

1. Heat oil in a large saucepan over medium-high heat. Add mushrooms and celery mixture; cook 6 to 7 minutes or until vegetables are browned, stirring occasionally.
2. While mushroom mixture cooks, prepare rice according to package directions, omitting salt and fat. Unwrap cheese; chop into bite-sized pieces.
3. Add milk, cheese, thyme, pepper, and salt to mushroom mixture, stirring well; bring to a boil. Reduce heat; cook 3 minutes or until cheese melts and soup thickens. Stir in rice. Cook 1 minute or until heated. **Yield:** 4 servings (serving size: 1 cup).

Per serving: CALORIES 214; FAT 9g (sat 3.4g, mono 2.9g, poly 0.6g); PROTEIN 14g; CARB 27.6g; FIBER 2.2g; CHOL 25mg; IRON 0.9mg; SODIUM 742mg; CALC 300mg

Mixed Greens and Raspberries with Hazelnuts and Raspberry Vinaigrette

prep: 5 minutes   *PointsPlus* value per serving: 5

3   tablespoons white balsamic raspberry vinegar (such as Alessi)
2   tablespoons extra-virgin olive oil
1   tablespoon honey
1   tablespoon water
¼   teaspoon salt
⅛   teaspoon freshly ground black pepper
1   (5-ounce) package spring mix (such as Fresh Express)
1½ cups raspberries
4   tablespoons coarsely chopped hazelnuts, toasted

1. Combine first 6 ingredients in a large bowl, stirring with a whisk. Add greens, tossing to coat.
2. Arrange salad on 4 plates; top evenly with berries and nuts. **Yield:** 4 servings (serving size: 1 cup salad, about ⅓ cup raspberries, and 1 tablespoon hazelnuts).

Per serving: CALORIES 181; FAT 13g (sat 2g, mono 8.3g, poly 1.7g); PROTEIN 2.9g; CARB 16.2g; FIBER 4.3g; CHOL 3mg; IRON 0.9mg; SODIUM 172mg; CALC 54mg

pictured on page 122

Spicy Poblano and Corn Soup

prep: 3 minutes • **cook:** 10 minutes   *PointsPlus* value per serving: 6

While we prefer poblano chile peppers, you may substitute green chiles instead.

1   (16-ounce) package frozen baby gold and white corn (such as Birds Eye), thawed and divided
2   cups fat-free milk, divided
4   poblano chiles, seeded and chopped (about 1 pound)
1   cup refrigerated prechopped onion
1   tablespoon water
¾   teaspoon salt
½   cup (2 ounces) reduced-fat shredded sharp cheddar cheese

1. Place 1 cup corn and 1½ cups milk in a Dutch oven. Bring mixture to a boil over medium heat.
2. Combine chopped chile, onion, and 1 tablespoon water in a microwave-safe bowl. Cover and microwave at HIGH 4 minutes.
3. Meanwhile, place remaining 2 cups corn and ½ cup milk in a blender; process until smooth. Add pureed mixture to corn mixture in pan. Stir in chile mixture and salt, and cook 6 minutes over medium heat. Ladle soup into bowls, and top each serving with 2 tablespoons cheddar cheese. **Yield:** 4 servings (serving size: about 1⅓ cups soup and 2 tablespoons cheese).

Per serving: CALORIES 239; FAT 4g (sat 2.2g, mono 0.3g, poly 0.5g); PROTEIN 13.2g; CARB 42.3g; FIBER 4.9g; CHOL 13mg; IRON 1.5mg; SODIUM 633mg; CALC 275mg

Menu
PointsPlus value
per serving: 8

Spicy Poblano and Corn Soup

1 (6-inch) whole-wheat flour
tortilla
PointsPlus value
per serving: 2

Game Plan

1. While milk and corn come
to a boil:
 • Seed and chop chile.

2. While onion and chile
microwave:
 • Puree remaining corn
 and milk.

3. Combine ingredients.

4. While soup cooks:
 • Cut tortilla into strips and
 toast.

Menu
PointsPlus value per serving: 7

Thai Coconut Shrimp Soup

16 rice crackers
PointsPlus value per serving: 2

Game Plan

1. Season and cook shrimp.

2. Sauté peppers.

3. Heat stock; add coconut milk and shrimp.

Thai Coconut Shrimp Soup

prep: 1 minute • **cook:** 13 minutes   **PointsPlus** value per serving: 5

Freshly squeezed lime juice is the secret ingredient in this recipe. It balances and brightens the flavors and adds just the right amount of tartness to the soup.

- 1   pound peeled and deveined large shrimp
- 1   tablespoon salt-free Thai seasoning (such as Frontier)
- Cooking spray
- 1   cup refrigerated prechopped tricolor bell pepper mix
- 2½ cups fat-free, lower-sodium chicken broth
- 1   tablespoon fish sauce
- 1   (13.5-ounce) can light coconut milk
- 1   tablespoon fresh lime juice
- Chopped fresh cilantro (optional)

1. Sprinkle shrimp with Thai seasoning; toss well. Heat a Dutch oven over medium-high heat; coat pan and shrimp with cooking spray. Add shrimp to pan; sauté 2 minutes or until shrimp are almost done. Remove shrimp from pan; set aside. Coat pan with cooking spray; add bell pepper, and sauté 2 minutes.

2. Add chicken broth and fish sauce to bell pepper in pan; bring to a boil. Reduce heat; simmer 5 minutes. Stir in coconut milk and reserved shrimp. Cook 2 minutes or until thoroughly heated. Remove from heat; stir in lime juice. Stir in cilantro, if desired. **Yield:** 4 servings (serving size: 1¾ cups).

Per serving: CALORIES 185; FAT 6g (sat 4.5g, mono 0.2g, poly 0.4g); PROTEIN 21.6g; CARB 12.4g; FIBER 0.6g; CHOL 168mg; IRON 4.3mg; SODIUM 858mg; CALC 38mg

pictured on page 121

Caldillo

prep: 4 minutes • **cook:** 45 minutes   *PointsPlus* value per serving: 4

Serve this spicy stew with peeled orange slices sprinkled with cinnamon sugar. Bottled cinnamon sugar can be found on the spice aisle of your local supermarket.

1   pound boneless sirloin steak (about ½ inch thick), cut into bite-sized pieces
    Cooking spray
1   (8-ounce) container refrigerated prechopped onion
3   cups water
2   (14½-ounce) cans diced tomatoes with zesty mild green chilies (such as Del Monte), undrained
1   teaspoon ground cumin
3   cups (½-inch) cubed unpeeled Yukon gold or red potato
¼   cup chopped fresh cilantro (optional)

1. Coat beef with cooking spray. Heat a large Dutch oven over high heat. Coat pan with cooking spray. Add beef to pan. Cook 3 minutes; stir in onion. Cook 5 minutes or until liquid evaporates and beef and onion are browned.

2. Stir in 3 cups water, tomatoes, and cumin; cover and bring to a boil. Reduce heat to medium; simmer 20 minutes. Add potato; cover and simmer 10 minutes or until potato is tender. Remove from heat; stir in cilantro, if desired. **Yield:** 6 servings (serving size: 1⅓ cups).

Per serving: CALORIES 165; FAT 3g (sat 1.2g, mono 1.6g, poly 0.2g); PROTEIN 18.3g; CARB 15.5g; FIBER 3.2g; CHOL 28mg; IRON 2mg; SODIUM 595mg; CALC 59mg

Menu
PointsPlus value per serving: 5

Caldillo

1 orange, segmented
PointsPlus value per serving: 0

1 teaspoon cinnamon sugar
PointsPlus value per serving: 1

Game Plan

1. As Dutch oven heats:
• Cut meat.

2. Brown beef and onion.

3. While soup cooks:
• Segment orange, and sprinkle with cinnamon sugar.

Menu
PointsPlus value
per serving: 8

Posole

1 (6-inch) whole-wheat flour
tortilla
PointsPlus value
per serving: 2

Game Plan

1. Brown pork.

2. Add hominy, tomatoes, and
water.

3. While soup comes to a boil:
• Cut and toast tortilla.
• Rinse and chop cilantro.

Posole

prep: 3 minutes • **cook:** 30 minutes   *PointsPlus* value per serving: 6

**The meat develops a rich, full-bodied flavor when it's cooked to a
dark brown, so be sure not to stir the pork until it releases easily
from the pan. Serve this fiery soup with warm flour tortillas.**

Cooking spray
1   (1-pound) pork tenderloin, trimmed and cut into bite-sized pieces
2   teaspoons salt-free Southwest chipotle seasoning blend (such as Mrs. Dash)
1   (15.5-ounce) can white hominy, undrained
1   (14.5-ounce) can Mexican-style stewed tomatoes with jalapeño peppers and
     spices (such as Del Monte), undrained
1   cup water
¼   cup chopped fresh cilantro

1. Heat a large saucepan over medium-high heat. Coat pan with cooking spray.
Sprinkle pork evenly with chipotle seasoning blend; coat evenly with cooking
spray. Add pork to pan; cook 4 minutes or until browned. Stir in hominy, tomatoes, and 1 cup water. Bring to a boil; cover, reduce heat, and simmer 20 minutes
or until pork is tender. Stir in cilantro. **Yield:** 4 servings (serving size: 1⅓ cups).

Per serving: CALORIES 233; FAT 5g (sat 1.4g, mono 1.9g, poly 0.8g); PROTEIN 24.4g; CARB 23g; FIBER 4.4g; CHOL 68mg; IRON 2.3mg; SODIUM 610mg;
CALC 33mg

Chicken Egg Drop Soup

prep: 4 minutes • **cook:** 9 minutes   *PointsPlus* value per serving: 5

Egg drop soup is noted for its strands of shredded egg. To achieve this characteristic look and texture, make sure you blend the egg mixture well, and stir it slowly into the broth.

     3½   cups fat-free, lower-sodium chicken broth
     1½   tablespoons lower-sodium soy sauce
      2   tablespoons cornstarch
      ¼   teaspoon freshly ground black pepper
      1   tablespoon water
      1   large egg
      1   large egg white
      2   cups chopped cooked chicken breast (about 8 ounces)
      ¼   cup chopped green onions (about 2)
      1   tablespoon dark sesame oil
      ¼   cup chopped cilantro (optional)

1. Combine broth and soy sauce in a medium saucepan. Bring to a boil over high heat. While broth mixture comes to a boil, combine cornstarch, pepper, and 1 tablespoon water in small bowl, stirring with a whisk until smooth. Gradually whisk cornstarch mixture into broth mixture. Reduce heat, and simmer, stirring frequently, 1 minute or until soup is slightly thick.
2. Combine egg and egg white, stirring with a whisk until blended. Slowly add egg mixture to soup, stirring gently. Add chicken, green onions, and sesame oil; cook 1 minute or until thoroughly heated.
3. Ladle soup evenly into 4 bowls; garnish with cilantro, if desired. **Yield:** 4 servings (serving size: 1¼ cups).

Per serving: CALORIES 203; FAT 7g (sat 1.5g, mono 2.7g, poly 2.1g); PROTEIN 27.3g; CARB 5.9g; FIBER 0.2g; CHOL 105mg; IRON 1.1mg; SODIUM 810mg; CALC 23mg

Menu
PointsPlus value per serving: 6

Chicken Egg Drop Soup

Asian Slaw

Game Plan

1. While broth mixture comes to a boil:
• Rinse and chop green onions.
• Assemble slaw.
• Combine cornstarch, pepper, and water.

2. Thicken soup.

3. Add beaten eggs, chicken, onions, and oil.

Asian Slaw

prep: 6 minutes   *PointsPlus* value per serving: 1

      ¼   cup reduced-fat mayonnaise
      1   tablespoon lower-sodium soy sauce
      1   teaspoon dark sesame oil
      4   cups packaged 3-color coleslaw (such as Fresh Express)
      ½   cup chopped fresh cilantro

1. Combine first 3 ingredients in a medium bowl, stirring with a whisk. Add coleslaw and cilantro; toss well. **Yield:** 4 servings (serving size: ¾ cup).

Per serving: CALORIES 46; FAT 3.2g (sat 0.2g, mono 0.5g, poly 1.5g); PROTEIN 0.8g; CARB 4.8g; FIBER 1.1g; CHOL 0mg; IRON 0.2mg; SODIUM 290mg; CALC 21mg

Menu

PointsPlus value
per serving: 7

Chicken-Vegetable Soup

1½-inch slice crusty French
bread
PointsPlus value
per serving: 2

Game Plan

1. While broth mixture comes
to a boil:
  • Heat vegetable-potato
    mixture.

2. Add seasonings to broth,
and boil.

3. Cut cooked vegetables, and
add to soup.

Chicken-Vegetable Soup

prep: 1 minute • **cook:** 14 minutes   *PointsPlus* value per serving: 5

If you use rotisserie chicken or refrigerated precooked chopped chicken, omit the salt in this recipe because the processed products are higher in sodium than home-cooked unsalted chicken.

  1   (32-ounce) carton fat-free, lower-sodium chicken broth
  2½ cups diced cooked chicken breast
  1   (8-ounce) container refrigerated prechopped celery, onion, and bell pepper mix
  1   cup frozen sliced carrot
  1   (14-ounce) package frozen baby potato and vegetable blend (such as Birds Eye)
  1   teaspoon bottled minced roasted garlic
  ½   teaspoon dried Italian seasoning
  ½   teaspoon curry powder
  ½   teaspoon freshly ground black pepper
  ¼   teaspoon salt
  1½ cups coarsely chopped fresh baby spinach
  1   (12-ounce) can evaporated fat-free milk
      Freshly ground black pepper (optional)

1. Bring first 4 ingredients to a boil in a covered large Dutch oven.

2. While broth mixture comes to a boil, place potato-vegetable blend in a microwave-safe bowl. Cover with heavy-duty plastic wrap; vent. Microwave at HIGH 5 minutes. While frozen vegetables cook, add garlic and next 4 ingredients to broth mixture; cover and continue to cook.

3. Using kitchen shears, snip cooked potato-vegetable blend into bite-sized pieces. Stir potato-vegetable blend, spinach, and milk into broth mixture. Cover and cook over high heat 5 minutes or until carrot is tender. Sprinkle with additional black pepper before serving, if desired. **Yield:** 6 servings (serving size: 1½ cups).

Per serving: CALORIES 208; FAT 2g (sat 0.6g, mono 0.7g, poly 0.5g); PROTEIN 25g; CARB 20g; FIBER 2.4g; CHOL 48mg; IRON 1.3mg; SODIUM 694mg; CALC 188mg

Chicken-Escarole Soup

prep: 1 minute • **cook:** 14 minutes   *PointsPlus* value per serving: 3

To cut down on time and keep cleanup to a minimum, use kitchen shears to easily chop tomatoes while they're still in the can.

1 (14½-ounce) can Italian-style stewed tomatoes, undrained and chopped
1 (14-ounce) can fat-free, lower-sodium chicken broth
2 cups coarsely chopped escarole (about 1 small head)
1 cup chopped cooked chicken breast
2 teaspoons extra-virgin olive oil

1. Combine tomatoes and broth in a large saucepan. Cover and bring to a boil over high heat. Reduce heat to low; simmer 5 minutes. Add escarole, chicken, and oil; cook 5 minutes. **Yield:** 4 servings (serving size: 1 cup).

Per serving: CALORIES 118; FAT 4g (sat 0.7g, mono 2.1g, poly 0.6g); PROTEIN 13.5g; CARB 7.9g; FIBER 1.5g; CHOL 30mg; IRON 1.1mg; SODIUM 535mg; CALC 49mg

Menu
PointsPlus value
per serving: 8

Chicken-Escarole Soup

Salad-Filled Focaccia

Game Plan

1. While tomatoes and broth come to a boil:
• Assemble salad.

2. After adding escarole, chicken, and oil:
• Top sliced focaccia with salad mixture.

Salad-Filled Focaccia

prep: 8 minutes   *PointsPlus* value per serving: 5

2½ cups mixed salad greens
⅓ cup refrigerated presliced red onion
3 tablespoons crumbled reduced-fat feta cheese
1 tablespoon fresh lemon juice
1 tablespoon extra-virgin olive oil
⅛ teaspoon crushed red pepper
1 (6-ounce) package focaccia, cut in half horizontally

1. Combine first 6 ingredients in a large bowl, tossing well to coat.
2. Arrange salad on bottom half of focaccia. Replace top half of loaf; cut crosswise into 4 equal portions. **Yield:** 4 servings (serving size: ¼ of filled focaccia).

Per serving: CALORIES 170; FAT 6g (sat 1.4g, mono 2.5g, poly 0.5g); PROTEIN 5.1g; CARB 25.2g; FIBER 1.3g; CHOL 4mg; IRON 1.5mg; SODIUM 347mg; CALC 36mg

pictured on page 123

Sausage and Barley Soup

prep: 5 minutes • **cook:** 18 minutes   *PointsPlus* value per serving: 4

Fresh, delicate baby spinach doesn't hold up to hours of cooking, so it is added at the last minute. Pureeing the vegetables allows you to drastically cut cooking time while maintaining all the rich flavors of the vegetables.

<table>
<tr><td></td><td>Cooking spray</td></tr>
<tr><td>6</td><td>ounces turkey breakfast sausage</td></tr>
<tr><td>2½</td><td>cups frozen bell pepper stir-fry (such as Birds Eye)</td></tr>
<tr><td>2</td><td>cups water</td></tr>
<tr><td>1</td><td>(14½-ounce) can Italian-style stewed tomatoes, undrained and chopped</td></tr>
<tr><td>¼</td><td>cup uncooked quick-cooking barley</td></tr>
<tr><td>1</td><td>cup coarsely chopped fresh baby spinach</td></tr>
</table>

1. Heat a large saucepan over medium-high heat. Coat pan with cooking spray. Add sausage; cook 3 minutes or until browned. Remove from heat.

2. While sausage cooks, place stir-fry and 2 cups water in a blender; process until smooth. Add stir-fry puree, tomatoes, and barley to sausage in pan. Bring mixture to a boil over high heat; cover, reduce heat to low, and simmer 10 minutes. Stir in spinach; cook 1 minute or until spinach wilts. **Yield:** 4 servings (serving size: 1½ cups).

Per serving: CALORIES 145; FAT 4g (sat 1.5g, mono 1.2g, poly 0.5g); PROTEIN 9.9g; CARB 17.9g; FIBER 2.6g; CHOL 33mg; IRON 1.6mg; SODIUM 493mg; CALC 53mg

Asiago-Topped Garlic Bread

prep: 6 minutes • **cook:** 4 minutes   *PointsPlus* value per serving: 3

<table>
<tr><td>1</td><td>garlic clove, pressed</td></tr>
<tr><td>1</td><td>(6-ounce) whole-wheat French bread baguette, cut in half lengthwise</td></tr>
<tr><td>1½</td><td>tablespoons light olive oil vinaigrette</td></tr>
<tr><td>½</td><td>teaspoon chopped fresh rosemary</td></tr>
<tr><td>¼</td><td>cup (1 ounce) finely grated Asiago cheese</td></tr>
</table>

1. Preheat broiler.

2. Spread garlic on cut sides of bread; brush evenly with vinaigrette. Top evenly with rosemary and cheese.

3. Broil 4 minutes or until cheese melts and bread is lightly browned. Cut into 8 pieces. **Yield:** 4 servings (serving size: 2 pieces).

Per serving: CALORIES 138; FAT 3g (sat 1.4g, mono 0.5g, poly 0.1g); PROTEIN 5.6g; CARB 20.2g; FIBER 0.7g; CHOL 7mg; IRON 1.1mg; SODIUM 283mg; CALC 70mg

---

Menu
PointsPlus value
per serving: 7

Sausage and Barley Soup

Asiago-Topped Garlic Bread

Game Plan

1. Preheat broiler.

2. While sausage cooks:
  • Puree stir-fry and water.

3. While puree, tomatoes, barley, and sausage come to a boil:
  • Assemble and broil garlic bread.

4. Add spinach to soup.

Side Dishes

Roasted Asparagus Caprese Toss

prep: 3 minutes • **cook:** 10 minutes   *PointsPlus* value per serving: 4

Bocconcini are small balls of fresh mozzarella—usually about 1 inch in diameter. If very thin asparagus spears are the only type available, we suggest cutting the mozzarella balls into fourths.

 2 pints cherry tomatoes
 1 pound asparagus, trimmed and cut into 1-inch pieces
 1 tablespoon olive oil
 ¼ teaspoon salt
 ¼ teaspoon freshly ground black pepper
 1 (7-ounce) container bocconcini, halved
 2 tablespoons coarsely chopped fresh basil

1. Preheat oven to 450°.

2. Place tomatoes and asparagus on a large rimmed baking sheet; drizzle with olive oil, and sprinkle with salt and pepper. Toss gently.

3. Bake at 450° for 10 to 12 minutes or until lightly browned and tender. Transfer vegetables to a large bowl. Add bocconcini; toss gently. Sprinkle with basil, and serve immediately. **Yield:** 6 servings (serving size: about ⅔ cup).

Per serving: CALORIES 140; FAT 10.2g (sat 5g, mono 1.7g, poly 0.4g); PROTEIN 7.3g; CARB 6g; FIBER 2.2g; CHOL 27mg; IRON 1.3mg; SODIUM 122mg; CALC 23mg

Gorgonzola Green Beans

prep: 3 minutes • **cook:** 16 minutes   *PointsPlus* value per serving: 2

 1 teaspoon olive oil
 2 cups vertically sliced sweet onion
 1 teaspoon sugar
 ½ teaspoon freshly ground black pepper
 2 (8-ounce) packages haricots verts
 ⅛ teaspoon salt
 ¼ cup (2 ounces) Gorgonzola cheese, crumbled

1. Heat oil in a medium skillet over medium heat. Add onion, sugar, and pepper. Cook 15 minutes or until onions are golden brown, stirring frequently.

2. While onion cooks, microwave haricots verts according to package directions. Remove beans from package; add beans and salt to onion. Cook 1 minute or until thoroughly heated. Transfer to a serving dish; sprinkle with cheese. Serve immediately. **Yield:** 6 servings (serving size: about ¾ cup).

Per serving: CALORIES 64; FAT 2.2g (sat 1.1g, mono 0.6g, poly 0.1g); PROTEIN 2.8g; CARB 9.7g; FIBER 3.2g; CHOL 4mg; IRON 0.9mg; SODIUM 121mg; CALC 63mg

White Bean Salad

prep: 10 minutes   *PointsPlus* value per serving: 3

Make this salad ahead and chill it, if desired. Hold out the arugula to add just before serving.

- 1 (15-ounce) can no-salt-added cannellini beans or other white beans, rinsed and drained
- 1 cup loosely packed baby arugula
- ¼ cup chopped celery leaves
- ¼ cup thinly sliced red onion
- ¼ cup (1 ounce) grated fresh Parmesan cheese
- 2 tablespoons chopped fresh parsley
- 1 teaspoon grated lemon rind
- 2 tablespoons fresh lemon juice
- 1 tablespoon extra-virgin olive oil
- ¼ teaspoon salt
- ¼ teaspoon freshly ground black pepper

1. Combine beans and next 3 ingredients in a medium bowl. Combine cheese and next 6 ingredients in a blender or food processor; process until blended. Pour dressing mixture over bean mixture, tossing to coat. **Yield:** 4 servings (serving size: ¾ cup).

Per serving: CALORIES 125; FAT 6.1g (sat 1.5g, mono 2.7g, poly 0.3g); PROTEIN 6.6g; CARB 11.3g; FIBER 3.2g; CHOL 5mg; IRON 1.1mg; SODIUM 295mg; CALC 137mg

Marinated Chickpea Salad

prep: 6 minutes   *PointsPlus* value per serving: 3

- 1 (15-ounce) can no-salt-added chickpeas (garbanzo beans), rinsed and drained
- ¼ cup chopped red bell pepper
- 2 tablespoons minced red onion
- 1 garlic clove, minced
- 2 tablespoons chopped fresh parsley
- 2 tablespoons cider vinegar
- 1 tablespoon olive oil
- ¼ teaspoon ground cumin
- ¼ teaspoon salt
- ¼ teaspoon freshly ground black pepper

1. Combine all ingredients in a medium bowl, tossing to coat. Cover and chill until ready to serve. **Yield:** 4 servings (serving size: ½ cup).

Per serving: CALORIES 111; FAT 4.1g (sat 0.5g, mono 2.7g, poly 0.3g); PROTEIN 4.1g; CARB 14g; FIBER 3.1g; CHOL 0mg; IRON 1mg; SODIUM 164mg; CALC 35mg

Spicy Broccoli with Almonds

prep: 4 minutes • **cook:** 6 minutes

PointsPlus value per serving: 3

Crushed red pepper kicks up the spice in this easy side. Tame the heat by decreasing to ¼ teaspoon.

  2   (12-ounce) packages broccoli florets
1½   tablespoons olive oil
  4   garlic cloves, minced
  ¾   teaspoon crushed red pepper
  ¼   teaspoon salt
  ¼   cup sliced almonds, toasted

1. Microwave broccoli according to package directions.
2. While broccoli cooks, heat oil in a large nonstick skillet over medium-high heat. Add garlic, red pepper, and salt; sauté 2 minutes. Add cooked broccoli to pan; sauté 3 minutes or until desired degree of doneness. Remove from heat, and sprinkle with almonds. **Yield:** 5 servings (serving size: 1 cup).

Per serving: CALORIES 115; FAT 6.4g (sat 0.7g, mono 4.4g, poly 1g); PROTEIN 2.8g; CARB 8.4g; FIBER 3.9g; CHOL 0mg; IRON 0.3mg; SODIUM 149mg; CALC 49mg

Crimson Slaw

prep: 10 minutes

PointsPlus value per serving: 5

Toss grilled chicken or pork into this sweet, tangy slaw to make a tasty filling for pitas or wraps.

  4   cups finely shredded red cabbage
  1   cup shredded carrot
  ¼   cup sweetened dried cranberries
  2   tablespoons grated orange rind
  ¼   cup strawberry balsamic vinaigrette (such as Maple Grove Farms)

1. Combine all ingredients in a large bowl; toss well. Serve immediately, or cover and chill until ready to serve. **Yield:** 4 servings (serving size: 1 cup).

Per serving: CALORIES 194; FAT 0.2g (sat 0g, mono 0g, poly 0.1g); PROTEIN 5.9g; CARB 46g; FIBER 11.9g; CHOL 0mg; IRON 2.4mg; SODIUM 315mg; CALC 133mg

Curried Cauliflower

prep: 5 minutes • **cook:** 7 minutes   *PointsPlus* value per serving: 3

2 (10-ounce) packages cauliflower florets
2 teaspoons olive oil
½ cup chopped onion
1 tablespoon minced peeled fresh ginger
2 garlic cloves, minced
¼ cup golden raisins
¼ cup organic vegetable broth
1 teaspoon curry powder
¼ teaspoon salt
¼ teaspoon freshly ground black pepper

1. Microwave cauliflower according to package directions. While cauliflower cooks, heat oil in a nonstick skillet over medium-high heat. Add onion, ginger, and garlic; sauté 3 minutes. Stir in raisins and next 4 ingredients. Cook 1 minute. Add cauliflower, tossing gently to coat. **Yield:** 4 servings (serving size: 1 cup).

Per serving: CALORIES 97; FAT 2.5g (sat 0.4g, mono 1.7g, poly 0.3g); PROTEIN 3.5g; CARB 18g; FIBER 4.5g; CHOL 0mg; IRON 1mg; SODIUM 226mg; CALC 47mg

Corn with Herbs, Lemon, and Queso Fresco

prep: 4 minutes • **cook:** 5 minutes   *PointsPlus* value per serving: 4

Cooking spray
2   garlic cloves, minced
2¾ cups frozen baby gold and white corn
¼   cup organic vegetable broth
¼   teaspoon salt
¼   teaspoon freshly ground black pepper
2   teaspoons olive oil
1   teaspoon grated lemon rind
1   teaspoon fresh lemon juice
1   teaspoon chopped fresh cilantro
½   teaspoon chopped fresh mint
¼   cup (1 ounce) crumbled queso fresco

1. Heat a large nonstick skillet over medium heat. Coat pan with cooking spray. Add garlic; sauté 1 minute or until tender. Add corn and next 3 ingredients. Cook 5 minutes or until corn is tender and liquid evaporates. Remove pan from heat. Combine oil and next 4 ingredients. Add to pan; toss well. Divide evenly among 4 dishes; sprinkle with queso fresco. **Yield:** 4 servings (serving size: ½ cup).

Per serving: CALORIES 151; FAT 4.8g (sat 1.1g, mono 2g, poly 0.3g); PROTEIN 5.1g; CARB 22.3g; FIBER 2.2g; CHOL 5mg; IRON 0.1mg; SODIUM 202mg; CALC 48mg

Browned Butter Pearled Couscous with Sage and Dried Cherries

prep: 1 minute • **cook:** 12 minutes   *PointsPlus* value per serving: 8

Earthy sage sizzles in the skillet with browned butter and provides background flavor for this quick-simmered side.

- 2   tablespoons butter
- 1   tablespoon chopped fresh sage, divided
- 1   cup Israeli couscous
- ½   cup dried cherries
- ¼   cup water
- ⅛   teaspoon salt

1. Melt butter in a large saucepan over medium-high heat; cook 3 minutes or until browned and fragrant. Add 2 teaspoons sage; sauté 1 minute. Add couscous and next 3 ingredients; bring to a boil. Cover, reduce heat, and simmer 8 minutes or until liquid is absorbed. Stir in remaining 1 teaspoon sage. **Yield:** 4 servings (serving size: ½ cup).

Per serving: CALORIES 312; FAT 6.3g (sat 3.7g, mono 1.5g, poly 0.2g); PROTEIN 6.6g; CARB 55.6g; FIBER 4g; CHOL 15mg; IRON 0.4mg; SODIUM 116mg; CALC 27mg

Edamame Pepper Stir-Fry

prep: 1 minute • **cook:** 7 minutes   *PointsPlus* value per serving: 3

Pineapple juice is the secret ingredient that gives this colorful mix of vegetables a sweet edge.

- 2   teaspoons dark sesame oil
- 1½ cups frozen shelled edamame (green soybeans)
- 1   (8-ounce) package refrigerated presliced tricolor bell peppers
- ¼   cup pineapple juice
- 1   tablespoon lower-sodium soy sauce

1. Heat oil in a large skillet over medium-high heat. Add edamame and bell pepper; sauté 5 minutes or until tender.
2. Add pineapple juice and soy sauce; cook 1 minute or until liquid almost evaporates. **Yield:** 4 servings (serving size: ¾ cup).

Per serving: CALORIES 117; FAT 5g (sat 0.4g, mono 0.9g, poly 1g); PROTEIN 8.2g; CARB 10g; FIBER 4g; CHOL 0mg; IRON 2.3mg; SODIUM 103mg; CALC 39mg

Roasted Italian Mushrooms

prep: 3 minutes • **cook:** 10 minutes   *PointsPlus* value per serving: 2

Cremini mushrooms are immature forms of portobello mushrooms usually labeled "baby portobellos" in the store.

- 2 (8-ounce) packages cremini mushrooms
- 1 tablespoon olive oil
- ½ teaspoon black pepper
- ½ cup chunky tomato, garlic, and onion pasta sauce (such as Ragú)
- 1 tablespoon capers
- 1 teaspoon grated lemon rind

1. Preheat oven to 450°.

2. Place mushrooms on a rimmed baking sheet. Drizzle with olive oil, and sprinkle with pepper. Bake at 450° for 10 minutes or until lightly browned.

3. While mushrooms roast, combine pasta sauce and next 2 ingredients in a 1-cup glass measure. Microwave at HIGH 30 seconds or until thoroughly heated.

4. Toss roasted mushrooms with sauce, and serve immediately. **Yield:** 4 servings (serving size: about ⅔ cup).

Per serving: CALORIES 91; FAT 4.4g (sat 0.5g, mono 2.7g, poly 0.4g); PROTEIN 3.4g; CARB 9.5g; FIBER 1.4g; CHOL 0mg; IRON 0.5mg; SODIUM 201mg; CALC 33mg

Stewed Okra and Tomatoes

prep: 10 minutes • **cook:** 20 minutes   *PointsPlus* value per serving: 2

A small amount of fried bacon goes a long way towards developing smoky goodness in this easy summer dish.

- 2 center-cut bacon slices
- ½ cup chopped onion
- 1 pound okra pods, trimmed and cut into ½-inch pieces
- 1 (14.5-ounce) can stewed tomatoes, undrained
- ½ cup water
- ¼ teaspoon salt
- ¼ teaspoon freshly ground black pepper
- Dash of hot sauce (optional)

1. Cook bacon in a Dutch oven over medium heat until crisp. Remove bacon from pan, reserving 1 teaspoon drippings in pan; crumble bacon, and set aside. Add onion to drippings in pan; sauté over medium-high heat 3 minutes or until tender.

2. Add okra, tomatoes with liquid, ½ cup water, salt, and pepper to pan. Bring to a boil; cover, reduce heat, and simmer 15 minutes or until okra is tender. Stir in hot sauce, if desired. Sprinkle with bacon. **Yield:** 4 servings (serving size: 1 cup).

Per serving: CALORIES 96; FAT 2.5g (sat 0.9g, mono 0.5g, poly 0.2g); PROTEIN 5g; CARB 16.3g; FIBER 5g; CHOL 5mg; IRON 2.3mg; SODIUM 452mg; CALC 132mg

Orzo and Zucchini Salad with Mint

prep: 4 minutes • **cook:** 9 minutes   *PointsPlus* value per serving: 4

Serve this chilled or at room temperature.

¾   cup uncooked orzo (rice-shaped pasta)
    Olive oil–flavored cooking spray
2¼ cups diced zucchini (about 2 small zucchini)
2   garlic cloves, minced
½   cup plain fat-free Greek yogurt
1   tablespoon chopped fresh mint
1   teaspoon white wine vinegar
1   teaspoon extra-virgin olive oil
¼   teaspoon salt
¼   teaspoon freshly ground black pepper

1. Cook orzo according to package directions, omitting salt and fat. Drain and rinse under cold water.
2. While orzo cooks, heat a large nonstick skillet over medium-high heat. Coat pan with cooking spray. Add zucchini and garlic. Cook 4 minutes or until tender. Remove from heat.
3. Combine yogurt and next 5 ingredients in a medium bowl; add orzo and zucchini mixture, tossing to coat. **Yield:** 4 servings (serving size: ½ cup).

Per serving: CALORIES 161; FAT 2.1g (sat 0.2g, mono 0.9g, poly 0.2g); PROTEIN 7.5g; CARB 28g; FIBER 2g; CHOL 0mg; IRON 0.3mg; SODIUM 163mg; CALC 34mg

Pesto Pasta Salad

prep: 5 minutes • **cook:** 10 minutes   *PointsPlus* value per serving: 6

This side salad makes enough to store in the fridge and take for lunch the next day.

1½ cups uncooked multigrain farfalle (bow tie pasta)
¼   cup refrigerated reduced-fat pesto with basil (such as Buitoni)
2   cups grape tomatoes, halved
¾   cup fresh mozzarella cheese, cubed
½   cup loosely packed fresh basil leaves, chopped
    Grated fresh Parmesan cheese (optional)

1. Cook pasta according to package directions, omitting salt and fat. Drain.
2. Toss pasta with pesto, tomatoes, and mozzarella cheese. Add basil, and toss gently. Sprinkle with Parmesan cheese, if desired. **Yield:** 8 servings (serving size: ½ cup).

Per serving: CALORIES 220; FAT 7.5g (sat 2.9g, mono 0g, poly 0g); PROTEIN 10.5g; CARB 27g; FIBER 3.4g; CHOL 16mg; IRON 1.8mg; SODIUM 91mg; CALC 26mg

Peas with Bacon, Onion, and Mushrooms

prep: 1 minute • **cook:** 10 minutes   *PointsPlus* value per serving: 4

 2   bacon slices
 ½   cup chopped onion
 1   (8-ounce) package fresh sliced mushrooms
 2   cups frozen petite peas
 2   tablespoons whipping cream
 ¼   teaspoon salt
 ¼   teaspoon freshly ground black pepper

1. Cook bacon in a large nonstick skillet over medium-high heat until crisp. Remove bacon from pan; crumble, and set aside.
2. Add onion and mushrooms to drippings in pan. Sauté 4 minutes or until tender. Add peas to pan; cook 2 minutes or until hot. Stir in cream, salt, pepper, and reserved bacon. Cook 1 minute or until sauce thickens. **Yield:** 4 servings (serving size: ¾ cup).

Per serving: CALORIES 163; FAT 8.1g (sat 3.5g, mono 3.1g, poly 0.7g); PROTEIN 6.6g; CARB 14.9g; FIBER 4.7g; CHOL 18mg; IRON 1.7mg; SODIUM 403mg; CALC 13mg

Orange-Scented Snow Peas

prep: 10 minutes • **cook:** 2 minutes   *PointsPlus* value per serving: 1

Fresh snow peas are best served crisp-tender. Fresh orange rind and juice give these just a hint of orange flavor.

 2   teaspoons brown sugar
 2   teaspoons lower-sodium soy sauce
 1   teaspoon grated orange rind
 ¼   cup fresh orange juice
 1   garlic clove, minced
 ½   teaspoon grated peeled fresh ginger
 ⅛   teaspoon salt
 ⅛   teaspoon freshly ground black pepper
 3   cups snow peas, trimmed

1. Combine first 8 ingredients in a large bowl; add snow peas, tossing well.
2. Heat a large nonstick skillet over medium-high heat. Add snow pea mixture; sauté 2 minutes or until crisp-tender and liquid almost evaporates. **Yield:** 4 servings (serving size: ½ cup).

Per serving: CALORIES 35; FAT 0.1g (sat 0g, mono 0g, poly 0.1g); PROTEIN 1.6g; CARB 7.2g; FIBER 1.3g; CHOL 0mg; IRON 1mg; SODIUM 140mg; CALC 25mg

Cheesy Scalloped Potatoes

prep: 11 minutes • **cook:** 20 minutes   *PointsPlus* value per serving: 4

  2   tablespoons all-purpose flour
  ½   teaspoon salt
  ⅛   teaspoon freshly ground black pepper
  2   cups 2% reduced-fat milk
  1½ cups (6 ounces) reduced-fat shredded extrasharp cheddar cheese, divided
  1½ pounds baking potatoes, peeled and cut into ⅛-inch-thick slices
      Cooking spray

1. Preheat broiler.
2. Combine first 3 ingredients in a large saucepan; gradually add milk, stirring with a whisk until smooth. Cook over medium-high heat, stirring constantly with a whisk, until thick and bubbly. Stir in 1 cup cheese, stirring until cheese melts.
3. Add potatoes to cheese sauce, stirring gently to coat. Spoon potatoes into an 11 x 7–inch microwaveable glass or ceramic baking dish coated with cooking spray. Cover with plastic wrap; microwave at HIGH 4 minutes. Vent, and microwave an additional 8 minutes or until potatoes are tender.
4. Remove baking dish from microwave; uncover. Sprinkle remaining ½ cup cheese over potatoes. Broil 1 to 2 minutes or just until cheese melts and edges are lightly browned. **Yield:** 10 servings (serving size: ½ cup).

Per serving: CALORIES 138; FAT 4.8g (sat 2.8g, mono 0.3g, poly 0.1g); PROTEIN 7.2g; CARB 17.7g; FIBER 1.3g; CHOL 16mg; IRON 0.3mg; SODIUM 279mg; CALC 305mg

Hash Brown Casserole

prep: 5 minutes • **cook:** 35 minutes   *PointsPlus* value per serving: 4

  1   (10¾-ounce) can reduced-fat, reduced-sodium cream of chicken soup
  1   cup (4 ounces) reduced-fat shredded sharp cheddar cheese
  ½   cup light sour cream
  ½   teaspoon salt
  4½ cups frozen shredded hash brown potatoes, thawed
      Cooking spray
  1   cup crushed cornflakes

1. Preheat oven to 350°.
2. Combine first 4 ingredients in a large bowl. Gently stir in potatoes.
3. Spoon potato mixture into an 8-inch square glass or ceramic baking dish coated with cooking spray. Top with cereal flakes, and coat cereal with cooking spray.
4. Bake at 350° for 35 minutes or until bubbly. **Yield:** 8 servings (serving size: ½ cup).

Per serving: CALORIES 141; FAT 5.6g (sat 3.1g, mono 0.6g, poly 0.2g); PROTEIN 6.1g; CARB 18.7g; FIBER 1.1g; CHOL 19mg; IRON 1.4mg; SODIUM 490mg; CALC 225mg

Roasted Lemon-Parsley Potatoes

prep: 4 minutes • **cook:** 17 minutes   ***PointsPlus* value per serving: 6**

    12   small red potatoes, halved (about 1½ pounds)
     2   teaspoons olive oil
     ¼   teaspoon freshly ground black pepper
    1½   tablespoons chopped fresh parsley
     ½   teaspoon grated lemon rind
     1   tablespoon fresh lemon juice
     ¼   teaspoon salt

1. Preheat oven to 450°.

2. Place potatoes in a bowl; drizzle with oil, and sprinkle with pepper, tossing to coat. Arrange potatoes in a single layer in a shallow roasting pan. Bake at 450° for 15 minutes; stir. Bake an additional 2 minutes or until browned and tender.

3. Spoon potatoes into a serving bowl; stir in parsley and remaining ingredients. **Yield:** 6 servings (serving size: ½ cup).

Per serving: CALORIES 213; FAT 2g (sat 0.3g, mono 1.2g, poly 0.3g); PROTEIN 5.4g; CARB 45g; FIBER 4.9g; CHOL 0mg; IRON 2.1mg; SODIUM 115mg; CALC 30mg

Bourbon-and-Brown Sugar– Glazed Sweet Potatoes

prep: 4 minutes • **cook:** 12 minutes   ***PointsPlus* value per serving: 5**

Bourbon puts a spin on this Thanksgiving favorite without adding a lot of calories.

     4   cups (½-inch) cubed peeled sweet potato (about 1½ pounds)
     ¼   cup packed light brown sugar
     1   tablespoon butter
     2   tablespoons bourbon
     ¼   teaspoon salt
     ¼   teaspoon freshly ground black pepper

1. Place sweet potatoes in a medium-sized microwave-safe bowl. Cover with plastic wrap; vent. Microwave at HIGH 10 minutes or until tender.

2. Combine brown sugar and butter in a large nonstick skillet over medium-high heat. Cook 1 minute or until melted and bubbly. Add bourbon; cook 30 seconds or until mixture thickens. Add sweet potatoes, salt, and pepper, stirring until potatoes are coated. **Yield:** 4 servings (serving size: ½ cup).

Per serving: CALORIES 209; FAT 3g (sat 1.9g, mono 0.8g, poly 0.1g); PROTEIN 2.2g; CARB 40g; FIBER 4g; CHOL 7mg; IRON 1mg; SODIUM 243mg; CALC 53mg

Basmati Rice with Grapes and Pine Nuts

prep: 1 minute • **cook:** 10 minutes   *PointsPlus* value per serving: 5

    2   teaspoons olive oil
    ½   cup prechopped red onion
    2   garlic cloves, minced
    1   (8.5-ounce) package microwaveable precooked basmati rice
    ½   teaspoon ground cumin
    ¼   teaspoon salt
    ¼   teaspoon freshly ground black pepper
    1   cup seedless red grapes, halved
    3   tablespoons chopped fresh parsley
    2   tablespoons pine nuts, toasted

1. Heat oil in a medium-sized nonstick skillet over medium-high heat. Add onion and garlic; sauté 3 to 4 minutes or until onion is almost tender. Stir in rice, cumin, salt, and pepper; sauté 2 minutes. Add grapes, and cook just until thoroughly heated. Add parsley and pine nuts; toss well. **Yield:** 4 servings.

Per serving: CALORIES 187; FAT 6.7g (sat 0.6g, mono 2.5g, poly 1.8g); PROTEIN 4g; CARB 30g; FIBER 1.5g; CHOL 0mg; IRON 1.5mg; SODIUM 156mg; CALC 28mg

Squash Casserole

prep: 12 minutes • **cook:** 38 minutes   *PointsPlus* value per serving: 3

        Cooking spray
    3   (10-ounce) packages refrigerated presliced yellow squash and zucchini mix
        (about 7 cups)
    1½ cups chopped onion
    ½   teaspoon salt
    ½   teaspoon freshly ground black pepper
    ½   cup light sour cream
    ½   cup (2 ounces) reduced-fat shredded sharp cheddar cheese
    ¾   cup panko (Japanese breadcrumbs)

1. Preheat oven to 400°.
2. Heat a large nonstick skillet over medium-high heat. Coat pan with cooking spray. Add squash mix, onion, salt, and pepper; cook 8 minutes or until tender, stirring occasionally. Stir in sour cream and cheese.
3. Spoon squash mixture into an 8-inch square glass or ceramic baking dish coated with cooking spray. Top with panko; coat panko with cooking spray. Bake at 400° for 30 minutes or until golden and bubbly. **Yield:** 6 servings (serving size: about ¾ cup).

Per serving: CALORIES 126; FAT 5.2g (sat 2.9g, mono 0.7g, poly 0.2g); PROTEIN 6.2g; CARB 15g; FIBER 2.5g; CHOL 14mg; IRON 0.7mg; SODIUM 306mg; CALC 127mg

Desserts

Strawberry Dessert Bruschetta

prep: 5 minutes

PointsPlus value per serving: 2

This sweet take on the savory tomato-topped appetizer is a great last-minute dessert suitable for entertaining.

- ½   cup (4 ounces) tub-style light cream cheese
- 2   tablespoons lemon curd
- 16   rectangular sugar cookies (such as Pepperidge Farm Bordeaux)
- 1   cup strawberries, coarsely chopped
- Fresh Mint sprigs (optional)

1. Combine cream cheese and lemon curd. Spread about 1 tablespoon cream cheese mixture on 1 side of each cookie. Top evenly with strawberries and, if desired, mint sprigs. Serve immediately. **Yield:** 16 servings (serving size: 1 bruschetta).

Per serving: CALORIES 57; FAT 2.4g (sat 1.4g, mono 1.2g, poly 0.1g); PROTEIN 1.2g; CARB 7.9g; FIBER 0.7g; CHOL 8mg; IRON 0.1mg; SODIUM 59mg; CALC 24mg

Orange Icebox Cookies

prep: 12 minutes • **cook:** 12 minutes • **other:** 1 hour
PointsPlus value per serving: 2

Icebox cookies are a great make-ahead dessert option. Keep the dough refrigerated until you are ready to slice, bake, and eat warm cookies!

¼   cup butter, softened
⅓   cup powdered sugar
⅛   teaspoon salt
1   large egg yolk
1   tablespoon grated orange rind
2   teaspoons orange juice
1   cup all-purpose flour

1. Beat butter with a mixer at medium speed until creamy. Add sugar and salt; beat until fluffy. Slowly add egg yolk, orange rind, and orange juice, beating until combined.
2. Lightly spoon flour into a dry measuring cup; level with a knife. Add to butter mixture, beating until blended. Shape dough into a 3-inch log. Wrap log in plastic wrap; chill 1 hour.
3. Preheat oven to 350°.
4. Unwrap dough roll. Slice with a sharp knife into 13 slices (about ¼ inch thick). Reshape into rounds, if necessary. Arrange slices 1 inch apart on a baking sheet lined with parchment paper. Bake at 350° for 12 minutes or until golden brown. Cool on a wire rack. **Yield:** 13 servings (serving size: 1 cookie).

Per serving: CALORIES 83; FAT 4g (sat 2.4g, mono 1.1g, poly 0.2g); PROTEIN 1.3g; CARB 10.6g; FIBER 0.3g; CHOL 26mg; IRON 0.5mg; SODIUM 48mg; CALC 5mg

pictured on page 127

Chewy Chocolate Cookies

prep: 7 minutes • **cook:** 17 minutes   *PointsPlus* value per serving: 2

These flourless chocolate cookies are unbelievably rich-tasting without the guilt!

  2   cups powdered sugar
  ½   cup unsweetened cocoa
  ¼   cup chopped walnuts, toasted
  1   tablespoon cornstarch
  ¼   teaspoon salt
  2   large egg whites, lightly beaten

1. Preheat oven to 300°.
2. Combine first 5 ingredients in a medium bowl. Add egg whites, stirring until combined (dough will be thick).
3. Shape dough into 21 (1-inch) balls. Arrange balls 1½ inches apart on baking sheets lined with parchment paper. Bake at 300° for 17 minutes or until cookies do not spring back when lightly touched. **Yield:** 21 servings (serving size: 1 cookie).

Per serving: CALORIES 61; FAT 1.2g (sat 0.3g, mono 0.2g, poly 0.7g); PROTEIN 1g; CARB 13g; FIBER 0.8g; CHOL 0mg; IRON 0.3mg; SODIUM 34mg; CALC 4mg

pictured on page 127

Dark Chocolate–Rice Cereal Treats

prep: 8 minutes • **cook:** 5 minutes • **other:** 1 hour and 15 minutes
PointsPlus value per serving: 4

All ages will go for these crisp cereal squares smothered with a soft chocolate topping.

    2   cups bittersweet chocolate chips, divided
    3   tablespoons light butter
    1   (10.5-ounce) package miniature marshmallows
    6   cups oven-toasted rice cereal (such as Rice Krispies)
    Cooking spray

1. Place 1 cup chocolate chips, butter, and marshmallows in a medium saucepan. Cook over medium heat 3 to 4 minutes or until melted, stirring frequently.
2. Combine cereal and butter mixture in a large bowl, tossing to coat. Spread mixture evenly in a 13 x 9–inch metal baking pan coated with cooking spray. Let stand 15 minutes.
3. Place remaining 1 cup chocolate chips in a microwave-safe bowl. Microwave at HIGH 1 minute, stirring after 30 seconds. Spread chocolate evenly over cereal mixture in pan. Let stand until cool (about 1 hour). Cut into squares. **Yield:** 24 servings (serving size: 1 square).

Per serving: CALORIES 144; FAT 6.3g (sat 3.6g, mono 0g, poly 0g); PROTEIN 1.6g; CARB 23.1g; FIBER 1g; CHOL 2mg; IRON 2.3mg; SODIUM 82mg; CALC 1mg

Ice Cream Candy Bars

prep: 6 minutes • **other:** 8 hours   *PointsPlus* value per serving: 3

This will remind you of a popular cone-shaped, ice cream–truck favorite!

     1   (8.4-ounce) package reduced-fat chocolate chip granola bars, unwrapped and
         crumbled (such as Quaker Chewy)
     2   cups butter pecan light ice cream (such as Edy's)
     ½   cup fat-free caramel topping
     ½   cup fat-free hot fudge topping
     ½   cup chopped dry-roasted peanuts

1. Line an 8-inch square metal baking pan with foil, allowing foil to extend over edge of pan. Press granola bars, in a single layer, into pan. Spread ice cream over granola bars. Drizzle caramel and hot fudge toppings over ice cream layer; sprinkle with peanuts.
2. Cover and freeze 8 hours or until firm. Carefully lift foil out of pan. Remove ice cream mixture from foil, and cut into bars. **Yield:** 16 servings (serving size: 1 bar).

Per serving: CALORIES 120; FAT 3.6g (sat 0.9g, mono 1.2g, poly 0.8g); PROTEIN 2.1g; CARB 19.7g; FIBER 0.4g; CHOL 5mg; IRON 0.1mg; SODIUM 87mg; CALC 23mg

pictured on page 127

Chewy Graham Cracker–Chocolate Chip Bars

prep: 5 minutes • **cook:** 25 minutes • **other:** 40 minutes
PointsPlus value per serving: 4

These chewy treats will quickly become a favorite—only three ingredients and a *PointsPlus* value per serving of 4.

    Cooking spray
1½ cups packaged graham cracker crumbs
½ cup semisweet chocolate minichips
1 (14-ounce) can low-fat sweetened condensed milk

1. Preheat oven to 350°.

2. Line a 9-inch square metal baking pan with foil, allowing foil to extend over edge of pan. Coat foil with cooking spray. Combine cracker crumbs and remaining ingredients in a large bowl, stirring with a wooden spoon until blended; spread into prepared pan.

3. Bake at 350° for 25 minutes or until golden brown. Carefully lift foil out of pan and place on a wire rack; cool completely on wire rack. Remove foil, and cut into bars. **Yield:** 16 servings (serving size: 1 bar).

Per serving: CALORIES 142; FAT 3.4g (sat 1.7g, mono 0.8g, poly 0.4g); PROTEIN 2.7g; CARB 24g; FIBER 0.5g; CHOL 3mg; IRON 0.5mg; SODIUM 74mg; CALC 67mg

Raspberry Pavlovas

prep: 15 minutes • **cook:** 1 hour and 30 minutes • **other:** 1 hour
PointsPlus value per serving: 4

The traditional version of this famous Australian dessert, named after Russian ballerina Anna Pavlova, consists of a crisp meringue base topped with whipped cream and fruit. Here, we use sweetened Greek yogurt instead of whipped cream for an equally impressive dessert.

  2   large egg whites
⅛ teaspoon cream of tartar
½ cup plus 1 tablespoon sugar, divided
¼ cup plain fat-free Greek yogurt
  1   cup fresh raspberries

1. Preheat oven to 225°.
2. Cover a large baking sheet with parchment paper. Draw 4 (3-inch) circles on paper. Turn paper over; secure onto baking sheet with masking tape.
3. Place egg whites and cream of tartar in a large bowl; beat with a mixer at high speed until foamy. Gradually add ½ cup sugar, 1 tablespoon at a time, beating until stiff peaks form.
4. Divide egg white mixture evenly among 4 drawn circles on baking sheet. Spread egg white mixture onto the circles using the back of a spoon.
5. Bake at 225° for 1½ hours or until dry. Turn oven off; cool meringues in closed oven 1 hour. Carefully remove meringues from paper.
6. Combine remaining 1 tablespoon sugar and yogurt in a small bowl. Divide among meringues, and top with raspberries. Serve immediately. **Yield:** 4 servings (serving size: 1 meringue, about ¼ cup raspberries, and 1 tablespoon yogurt mixture).

Per serving: CALORIES 141; FAT 0.2g (sat 0g, mono 0g, poly 0.1g); PROTEIN 3.4g; CARB 32.8g; FIBER 2g; CHOL 0mg; IRON 0.2mg; SODIUM 33mg; CALC 19mg

Raspberry–Cheesecake Mousse Parfaits

prep: 8 minutes • **other:** 5 minutes *PointsPlus* value per serving: 6

Jump-start this company-worthy dessert by chilling the sweetened condensed milk several hours before preparing. It helps the mousse set quickly.

1 (14-ounce) can fat-free sweetened condensed milk
½ cup fat-free milk
1 (3.9-ounce) package cheesecake instant pudding mix
2 cups fresh raspberries
2 teaspoons sugar
1 (8-ounce) container frozen fat-free whipped topping, thawed
10 tablespoons cinnamon graham cracker crumbs (about 2½ cookie sheets)

1. Combine condensed milk and fat-free milk in a large bowl, stirring with a whisk until smooth. Add pudding mix; stir with a whisk 2 minutes. Cover and chill 5 minutes.

2. While pudding mixture chills, combine raspberries and sugar. Fold whipped topping into pudding mixture. Spoon about ⅓ cup pudding mixture into bottom of each of 10 parfait glasses. Top each serving with about 1½ tablespoons raspberries and 1½ teaspoons graham cracker crumbs. Repeat layers with remaining pudding mixture, raspberries, and crumbs. **Yield:** 10 servings (serving size: 1 parfait).

Per serving: CALORIES 251; FAT 0.7g (sat 0.1g, mono 0.2g, poly 0.3g); PROTEIN 4.6g; CARB 54.1g; FIBER 1.8g; CHOL 6mg; IRON 0.4mg; SODIUM 249mg; CALC 139mg

pictured on page 126

Mini Turtle Trifles

prep: 12 minutes   *PointsPlus* value per serving: 9

Enjoy this dessert using Weight Watchers treats you may already have around the house.

- 2 (3.75-ounce) cups refrigerated vanilla sugar-free, reduced-calorie pudding snacks
- 1 ounce dark chocolate, melted
- 2 (2.3-ounce) double chocolate muffins (such as Weight Watchers)
- ¼ cup fat-free caramel topping
- ½ cup frozen fat-free whipped topping, thawed
- 4 (0.5-ounce) pecan crown candies, chopped (such as Weight Watchers)

1. Combine pudding and melted chocolate, stirring with a whisk until blended. Coarsely crumble one-fourth of a muffin into each of 4 dessert dishes or wide-bowl wine glasses. Drizzle each serving with 1½ teaspoons caramel topping. Top each serving with 1 heaping tablespoon pudding mixture and 2 tablespoons whipped topping. Repeat layers. Sprinkle each serving with a chopped pecan candy. **Yield:** 4 servings (serving size: 1 trifle).

Per serving: CALORIES 322; FAT 8.8g (sat 5g, mono 0g, poly 0g); PROTEIN 3g; CARB 62.2g; FIBER 7.6g; CHOL 12mg; IRON 2.1mg; SODIUM 300mg; CALC 70mg

Lemon-Lime Angel Food Snack Cake

prep: 8 minutes • **cook:** 35 minutes   *PointsPlus* value per serving: 4

Baking an angel food cake in a rectangular pan versus the traditional tube pan eliminates the long cooling time and tricky removal from the pan.

    Cooking spray
  1 lemon
  1 lime
  1 (16-ounce) package angel food cake mix
  1½ cups powdered sugar

1. Preheat oven to 350°. Coat bottom of a 13 x 9–inch metal baking pan with cooking spray; set aside.

2. Grate 1½ teaspoons rind each from lemon and lime; squeeze 2 tablespoons juice from each.

3. Prepare batter for angel food cake according to package directions; fold in ½ teaspoon of each rind. Spoon batter into prepared pan. Bake at 350° for 35 minutes or until a wooden pick inserted in center comes out clean.

4. Combine powdered sugar, remaining 2 teaspoons rind, and juices, stirring until smooth. Pierce top of cake with a wooden skewer 15 to 20 times; pour glaze over cake, allowing glaze to soak into holes. **Yield:** 16 servings (serving size: 1 piece).

Per serving: CALORIES 151; FAT 0.1g (sat 0g, mono 0g, poly 0.1g); PROTEIN 2.5g; CARB 35.7g; FIBER 0.1g; CHOL 0mg; IRON 0.1mg; SODIUM 209mg; CALC 35mg

Lemon Summer Pudding

prep: 9 minutes • **other:** 4 hours   *PointsPlus* value per serving: 5

Serve this refreshing light and lemony summer cake with any fresh berry.

   1   lemon
   1   cup vanilla low-fat yogurt
   2   tablespoons honey, divided
   1   (15-ounce) angel food cake, cut into 1-inch cubes
   2   cups sliced strawberries

1. Line an 8 x 4–inch loaf pan with plastic wrap.

2. Grate 1 teaspoon rind from lemon; squeeze juice to measure 2 tablespoons. Combine yogurt, lemon juice, lemon rind, and 1 tablespoon honey in a large bowl, stirring well with a whisk. Add cake cubes, and toss to coat well.

3. Transfer cake mixture to prepared pan; gently press down, and cover with plastic wrap. Chill 4 hours.

4. While cake chills, combine strawberries and remaining 1 tablespoon honey.

5. Unmold cake, and remove plastic wrap. Cut into 8 slices; serve with strawberries. **Yield:** 8 servings (serving size: 1 slice cake and ¼ cup strawberries).

Per serving: CALORIES 198; FAT 0.9g (sat 0.3g, mono 0.1g, poly 0.3g); PROTEIN 4.5g; CARB 44.5g; FIBER 1.7g; CHOL 2mg; IRON 0.5mg; SODIUM 418mg; CALC 120mg

Creamy Vanilla-Blueberry Pie

prep: 9 minutes • **cook:** 2 minutes • **other:** 4 hours
PointsPlus value per serving: 7

The secret ingredient in this pie is coffee creamer—it adds creaminess and lots of vanilla essence in just one ingredient.

- 2   teaspoons unflavored gelatin
- ¾   cup fat-free French vanilla liquid non-dairy creamer (such as Coffee-mate), divided
- 2   (8-ounce) blocks ⅓-less-fat cream cheese, softened
- 1   (9.5-ounce) jar blueberry spread (such as Dickinson's Purely Fruit)
- 1   (6-ounce) shortbread crust (such as Keebler's Ready Crust)
- Frozen fat-free whipped topping, thawed (optional)
- Fresh blueberries (optional)

1. Sprinkle gelatin over ¼ cup creamer in a small saucepan; let stand 1 minute. Cook over low heat 2 minutes, stirring until gelatin dissolves.

2. Beat cream cheese with a mixer at medium speed until smooth. Add blueberry spread; beat well. Gradually add gelatin mixture and remaining ½ cup creamer, beating until smooth. Pour mixture into crust. Cover and chill 4 hours. Top each slice with whipped topping and fresh blueberries, if desired. **Yield:** 12 servings (serving size: 1 slice).

Per serving: CALORIES 247; FAT 11.5g (sat 6.1g, mono 3.6g, poly 0.4g); PROTEIN 5.1g; CARB 29.6g; FIBER 0g; CHOL 27mg; IRON 0mg; SODIUM 242mg; CALC 27mg

Fresh Strawberry Pie

prep: 6 minutes • **cook:** 19 minutes • **other:** 4 hours
PointsPlus value per serving: 6

Make this pie during late spring and early summer when strawberries are plentiful and at their flavor peak.

  ½ (15-ounce) package refrigerated pie dough (such as Pillsbury)
  2 (16-ounce) packages strawberries, hulled and divided
  ½ cup sugar
  2 tablespoons cornstarch
  ⅓ cup (3 ounces) tub-style light cream cheese

1. Preheat oven to 450°.

2. Unroll dough, and fit into a 9-inch pie plate. Fold edges under, and flute; pierce bottom and sides of dough with a fork. Bake at 450° for 4 minutes or until lightly browned. Cool on a wire rack.

3. While crust bakes, place 1 package strawberries in a blender; process until smooth. Combine sugar and cornstarch in a large saucepan, stirring with a whisk; add pureed strawberries, and stir until blended. Bring mixture just to a boil; reduce heat, and simmer 3 minutes.

4. Spread cream cheese in bottom of cooled crust. Arrange remaining strawberries, hulled sides down, in crust. Pour pureed strawberry mixture over strawberries in crust; cover and chill at least 4 hours. **Yield:** 8 servings (serving size: 1 slice).

Per serving: CALORIES 214; FAT 8.3g (sat 3.8g, mono 3g, poly 1.1g); PROTEIN 2.7g; CARB 34.9g; FIBER 2.3g; CHOL 8mg; IRON 0.5mg; SODIUM 181mg; CALC 52mg

pictured on page 125

Fresh Berries with Limoncello-Mint Cream

prep: 6 minutes   *PointsPlus* value per serving: 5

A small amount of buttery rich mascarpone cheese gives this dessert sauce its silky texture. If you don't have limoncello on hand, use 1 tablespoon lemon juice plus ½ teaspoon grated lemon rind, and increase the sugar to 1 teaspoon.

- 3 tablespoons tub-style light cream cheese
- 2 tablespoons mascarpone cheese
- 2 tablespoons fat-free half-and-half
- 1 tablespoon limoncello
- ½ teaspoon sugar
- 1 tablespoon chopped fresh mint
- 3 cups mixed fresh berries
- 4 rectangular sugar cookies (such as Pepperidge Farm Bordeaux)

1. Combine first 5 ingredients in a small bowl, stirring with a whisk until smooth. Stir in mint. Spoon ¾ cup berries into each of 4 dishes; top evenly with limoncello cream. Serve with a cookie. **Yield:** 4 servings (serving size: ¾ cup berries, 2 tablespoons limoncello cream, and 1 cookie).

Per serving: CALORIES 179; FAT 9.4g (sat 5g, mono 0.1g, poly 0.2g); PROTEIN 3.2g; CARB 20.2g; FIBER 4g; CHOL 24mg; IRON 0.6mg; SODIUM 80mg; CALC 69mg

Black Bottom Chocolate Pots de Crème

prep: 6 minutes • **cook:** 33 minutes   *PointsPlus* value per serving: 7

Each of these rich baked puddings has a special surprise on the bottom—a crushed gooey chocolate-marshmallow cookie.

     1 cup 1% low-fat milk
     ⅓ cup sugar
     ⅛ teaspoon salt
     ⅓ cup bittersweet chocolate chips
     1 large egg
     1 large egg white
     8 devil's food cookie cakes (such as SnackWell's), coarsely crushed
     Cooking spray
     Frozen reduced-calorie whipped topping, thawed (optional)
     ½ ounce bittersweet chocolate, shaved (optional)

1. Preheat oven to 325°.
2. Combine first 3 ingredients in a medium saucepan. Cook over medium heat 3 minutes or until sugar dissolves, stirring frequently. Add chocolate chips, stirring until chocolate melts.
3. Combine egg and egg white in a medium bowl, stirring with a whisk. Gradually add hot milk mixture to eggs, stirring constantly with a whisk. Divide crushed cookies evenly among 4 (4-ounce) ramekins coated with cooking spray, pressing firmly to make a crust.
4. Pour custard evenly over crushed cookies. Place ramekins in a 13 x 9–inch metal baking pan; add hot water to pan to a depth of 1 inch. Bake at 325° for 30 minutes or until center barely moves when ramekin is touched. Remove ramekins from pan; cool completely on a wire rack. Serve immediately, or cover and chill until ready to serve. Top with whipped topping and shaved chocolate before serving, if desired. **Yield:** 4 servings (serving size: 1 ramekin).

Per serving: CALORIES 250; FAT 5.1g (sat 2.3g, mono 0.8g, poly 0.2g); PROTEIN 7g; CARB 47.5g; FIBER 0.5g; CHOL 56mg; IRON 1.2mg; SODIUM 181mg; CALC 80mg

Rum Raisin Vanilla Bean Pudding

prep: 1 minute • **cook:** 8 minutes • **other:** 5 minutes
PointsPlus value per serving: 6

You'll love the velvety texture of this popular ice cream flavor-turned-pudding.

   2 cups fat-free half-and-half, divided
   1 vanilla bean, split lengthwise
   ⅓ cup sugar
   3 tablespoons cornstarch
   2 large egg yolks, lightly beaten
   ½ cup raisins
   2 tablespoons dark rum

1. Place 1¾ cups half-and-half in a large microwave-safe bowl. Scrape seeds from vanilla bean into bowl; add bean to bowl. Microwave at HIGH 4 minutes. Remove and discard vanilla bean.

2. Combine sugar, cornstarch, and egg yolks in a large saucepan, stirring with a whisk; stir in remaining ¼ cup half-and-half. Gradually add half of hot milk to sugar mixture, stirring constantly with a whisk. Add remaining hot milk mixture to pan; bring to a boil. Cook 1 minute, stirring constantly with a whisk. Remove from heat. Stir in raisins and rum.

3. Pour pudding into a bowl. Place bowl in a large ice-water bath. Stir pudding 5 minutes or until completely cooled. Serve immediately, or cover surface of pudding with plastic wrap, and chill until ready to serve. **Yield:** 4 servings (serving size: about ½ cup).

Per serving: CALORIES 265; FAT 2.3g (sat 0.8g, mono 1g, poly 0.4g); PROTEIN 1.9g; CARB 49g; FIBER 0.7g; CHOL 105mg; IRON 0.6mg; SODIUM 127mg; CALC 100mg

Triple Grape Granita

prep: 6 minutes • **other:** 4 hours   *PointsPlus* value per serving: 2

Traditional granitas are usually made with fruit juices instead of the whole fruit. This refreshing dessert is a great way to sneak fiber and a fruit serving into your diet.

1   cup seedless red grapes
1   cup seedless green grapes
1   cup Concord grape juice
1   cup apple juice

1. Place all ingredients in a blender; process until smooth. Pour into an 8-inch square metal baking pan.
2. Cover and freeze 4 hours or until firm. Remove mixture from freezer; scrape entire mixture with a fork until fluffy. **Yield:** 6 servings (serving size: 1 cup).

Per serving: CALORIES 74; FAT 0.1g (sat 0g, mono 0g, poly 0g); PROTEIN 0.4g; CARB 19g; FIBER 0.5g; CHOL 0mg; IRON 0.2mg; SODIUM 2.7mg; CALC 8mg

Mexican Ice Cream Snowballs

prep: 10 minutes • **other:** 30 minutes   *PointsPlus* value per serving: 8

Traditional Mexican ingredients are highlighted in these fun frozen ice cream truffles. Make the whole batch, and keep them in the freezer to enjoy whenever you're craving something sweet.

¾ cup flaked sweetened coconut, toasted
½ cup unsalted pumpkinseed kernels or pine nuts, toasted
¼ teaspoon ground cinnamon
2 cups coffee light ice cream
¼ cup sugar-free, fat-free hot fudge sauce (such as Smucker's), heated

1. Combine first 3 ingredients in a shallow dish. Using a 1½-tablespoon ice cream scoop, divide ice cream into 18 balls. Roll each ball in coconut mixture. Place ice cream balls on a rimmed baking sheet; drizzle evenly with hot fudge sauce. Freeze 30 minutes or until firm. **Yield:** 6 servings (serving size: 3 ice cream balls).

Per serving: CALORIES 284; FAT 12.9g (sat 6.5g, mono 3.1g, poly 2.6g); PROTEIN 6.8g; CARB 37g; FIBER 1.9g; CHOL 43mg; IRON 2.5mg; SODIUM 102mg; CALC 74mg

Frozen Peppermint Hot Chocolate

prep: 6 minutes • **cook:** 2 minutes • **other:** 10 minutes
PointsPlus value per serving: 7

Think of this treat as a cross between hot chocolate and a milkshake.

  16   crème de menthe chocolaty mint thins, chopped
   1   (0.55-ounce) package sugar-free hot chocolate mix
1½   cups 1% low-fat milk, divided
1½   cups chocolate light ice cream
 ¼   cup frozen fat-free whipped topping, thawed
Fat-free chocolate syrup (such as Hershey's) (optional)
Additional chopped crème de menthe chocolaty mint thins (optional)

1. Combine chopped mints, hot chocolate mix, and ½ cup milk in a small sauce-pan. Cook over medium heat 1½ minutes or until chocolate melts and mixture is smooth, stirring constantly with a whisk. Cover and chill 10 minutes.

2. Combine cooled chocolate mixture, remaining 1 cup milk, and ice cream in a blender; process until smooth. Pour mixture into 4 glasses. Top each with 1 table-spoon whipped topping, and, if desired, chocolate syrup and additional chopped mints. **Yield:** 4 servings (serving size: ¾ cup).

Per serving: CALORIES 243; FAT 10.3g (sat 7.8g, mono 0.3g, poly 0g); PROTEIN 6.8g; CARB 31.5g; FIBER 1g; CHOL 20mg; IRON 0.2mg; SODIUM 128mg; CALC 242mg

pictured on page 124

Banana Pudding Ice Cream Smash

prep: 8 minutes • **other:** 2 hours   *PointsPlus* value per serving: 5

Bring the flair of a gourmet ice cream parlor to your own kitchen with banana pudding ingredients used as easy ice cream stir-ins.

  2 cups French vanilla low-fat ice cream, slightly softened
12 reduced-calorie vanilla wafers, broken into pieces
  2 small ripe bananas, sliced
 ¼ cup frozen fat-free whipped topping, thawed

1. Using two large spoons, combine ice cream and vanilla wafer pieces in a large bowl, mashing to blend. Add sliced banana, stirring just until blended. Cover and freeze 2 hours.
2. Spoon ice cream mixture evenly into 4 dishes; top evenly with whipped topping. Serve immediately. **Yield:** 4 servings (serving size: ½ cup).

Per serving: CALORIES 192; FAT 4.4g (sat 2.1g, mono 1.1g, poly 0.2g); PROTEIN 3.9g; CARB 36g; FIBER 1.3g; CHOL 20mg; IRON 0.4mg; SODIUM 87mg; CALC 63mg

Broiled Baby Doughnut Sundaes

prep: 4 minutes • **cook:** 2 minutes   *PointsPlus* value per serving: 4

Who knew broiled doughnuts would become an indulgent brûléed dessert idea? Use your favorite flavor light ice cream or frozen yogurt. We prefer vanilla with these crisp-edged doughnuts.

    12   miniature powdered sugar doughnuts
         Butter-flavored cooking spray
     ¾   cup vanilla light ice cream (such as Edy's)
     ¼   cup fat-free chocolate sundae syrup

1. Preheat broiler.

2. Gently cut doughnuts in half horizontally with a serrated bread knife; lightly coat cut sides with cooking spray. Place doughnuts, cut sides up, on a baking sheet coated with cooking spray. Broil doughnut halves on top oven rack 2 minutes or until browned.

3. Place 4 doughnut halves on each of 6 plates. Top each pair with 1 rounded tablespoon ice cream and 1 teaspoon chocolate syrup. **Yield:** 6 servings (serving size: 4 doughnut halves, 2 tablespoons ice cream, and 2 teaspoons chocolate syrup).

Per serving: CALORIES 163; FAT 5.4g (sat 1.6g, mono 0.2g, poly 0g); PROTEIN 2.6g; CARB 25.9g; FIBER 0.6g; CHOL 14mg; IRON 0.5mg; SODIUM 117mg; CALC 37mg

pictured on page 128

Pineapple-Macadamia Sundaes

prep: 4 minutes • **cook:** 10 minutes   *PointsPlus* value per serving: 6

A small amount of caramel topping stirred into melted brown sugar creates a yummy warm syrup for this fruity sundae. Purchase peeled and cored pineapple for easy slicing.

　4　(½-inch-thick) slices fresh pineapple
　　Butter-flavored cooking spray
　¼　cup packed brown sugar
　2　tablespoons fat-free caramel topping (such as Smucker's)
1⅓　cups pineapple sherbet
　2　tablespoons chopped macadamia nuts, toasted

1. Drain 2 tablespoons juice from pineapple container. Heat a large nonstick skillet over medium-high heat. Coat pan with cooking spray. Add pineapple to pan; cook 2 to 3 minutes on each side or until lightly browned. Add brown sugar and reserved pineapple juice; cook 2 minutes or until sugar melts and coats pineapple.
2. Remove pineapple from pan; place 1 pineapple slice on each of 4 plates. Add caramel topping to sugar in pan, stirring until smooth. Spoon ⅓ cup sherbet into center of each pineapple slice. Spoon brown sugar mixture evenly over sherbet; sprinkle with nuts. **Yield:** 4 servings (serving size: 1 pineapple slice, ⅓ cup sherbet, 1 tablespoon sauce, and 1½ teaspoons nuts).

Per serving: CALORIES 219; FAT 3.4g (sat 0.5g, mono 2.5g, poly 0.1g); PROTEIN 0.6g; CARB 46.5g; FIBER 1g; CHOL 0mg; IRON 0.3mg; SODIUM 49mg; CALC 36mg

Caramel–Kettle Corn Ice Cream Cups

prep: 8 minutes

PointsPlus value per serving: 7

This salty, sweet, gooey topping is a spin on the nostalgic and familiar popcorn treat in a box.

    1   (1.2-ounce) package 94% fat-free microwave kettle corn popcorn (such as Orville Redenbacher's)
    ¼   cup coarsely chopped lightly salted, dry-roasted peanuts
    2   tablespoons fat-free caramel topping
    1⅓ cups vanilla light ice cream
    4   (0.4-ounce) waffle bowls

1. Microwave popcorn according to package directions; set aside 1 cup for ice cream cups. Reserve remaining popcorn for another use.

2. Combine peanuts, 1 cup popcorn, and caramel topping, stirring until nuts are coated. Spoon ⅓ cup ice cream into each waffle bowl. Spoon ¼ cup popcorn mixture over each ice cream scoop, lightly pressing into ice cream to form a "shell." Serve immediately. **Yield:** 4 servings (serving size: 1 waffle bowl, ⅓ cup ice cream, and ¼ cup popcorn mixture).

Per serving: CALORIES 261; FAT 10.3g (sat 3.6g, mono 4g, poly 1.7g); PROTEIN 6.5g; CARB 37.5g; FIBER 2g; CHOL 27mg; IRON 1.5mg; SODIUM 241mg; CALC 104mg

Index

10 Simple Side Dishes

Vegetable	Servings	Preparation	Cooking Instructions
Asparagus	3 to 4 per pound	Snap off tough ends. Remove scales, if desired.	To steam: Cook, covered, on a rack above boiling water 2 to 3 minutes. To boil: Cook, covered, in a small amount of boiling water 2 to 3 minutes or until crisp-tender.
Broccoli	3 to 4 per pound	Remove outer leaves and tough ends of lower stalks. Wash; cut into spears.	To steam: Cook, covered, on a rack above boiling water 5 to 7 minutes or until crisp-tender.
Carrots	4 per pound	Scrape; remove ends, and rinse. Leave tiny carrots whole; slice large carrots.	To steam: Cook, covered, on a rack above boiling water 8 to 10 minutes or until crisp-tender. To boil: Cook, covered, in a small amount of boiling water 8 to 10 minutes or until crisp-tender.
Cauliflower	4 per medium head	Remove outer leaves and stalk. Wash. Break into florets.	To steam: Cook, covered, on a rack above boiling water 5 to 7 minutes or until crisp-tender.
Corn	4 per 4 large ears	Remove husks and silks. Leave corn on the cob, or cut off kernels.	Cook, covered, in boiling water to cover 8 to 10 minutes (on cob) or in a small amount of boiling water 4 to 6 minutes (kernels).
Green beans	4 per pound	Wash; trim ends, and remove strings. Cut into 1½-inch pieces.	To steam: Cook, covered, on a rack above boiling water 5 to 7 minutes. To boil: Cook, covered, in a small amount of boiling water 5 to 7 minutes or until crisp-tender.
Potatoes	3 to 4 per pound	Scrub; peel, if desired. Leave whole, slice, or cut into chunks.	To boil: Cook, covered, in boiling water to cover 30 to 40 minutes (whole) or 15 to 20 minutes (slices or chunks). To bake: Bake at 400° for 1 hour or until done.
Snow peas	4 per pound	Wash; trim ends, and remove tough strings.	To steam: Cook, covered, on a rack above boiling water 2 to 3 minutes. Or sauté in cooking spray or 1 teaspoon oil over medium-high heat 3 to 4 minutes or until crisp-tender.
Squash, summer	3 to 4 per pound	Wash; trim ends, and slice or chop.	To steam: Cook, covered, on a rack above boiling water 6 to 8 minutes. To boil: Cook, covered, in a small amount of boiling water 6 to 8 minutes or until crisp-tender.
Squash, winter *(including acorn, butternut, and buttercup)*	2 per pound	Rinse; cut in half, and remove all seeds. Leave in halves to bake, or peel and cube to boil.	To boil: Cook cubes, covered, in boiling water 20 to 25 minutes. To bake: Place halves, cut sides down, in a shallow baking dish; add ½ inch water. Bake, uncovered, at 375° for 30 minutes. Turn and season, or fill; bake an additional 20 to 30 minutes or until tender.